P9-DNX-349

KEYS TO INVESTING IN OPTIONS AND FUTURES

Third Edition

Nicholas G. Apostolou, DBA, CPA
U. J. LeGrange Endowed Professor
Louisiana State University

Barbara Apostolou, Ph.D., CPA
Arthur Andersen Distinguished Professor
Louisiana State University

BARRON'S

© Copyright 2000 by Barron's Educational Series, Inc.
Prior editions © Copyright 1991, 1995 by Barron's Educational Series, Inc.

All inquiries should be addressed to:
Barron's Educational Series, Inc.
250 Wireless Boulevard
Hauppauge, NY 11788
http://www.barronseduc.com

Library of Congress Catalog Card Number 99-56821

International Standard Book Number 0-7641-1303-8

Library of Congress Cataloging-in-Publication Data

Apostolou, Nicholas G.
        Keys to investing in options and futures / Nicholas G. Apostolou, Barbara
Apostolou. — 3rd ed.
            p.   cm. — (Barron's business keys)
        Includes index.
        ISBN 0-7641-1303-8
        1. Options (Finance) 2. Futures.   I. Apostolou, Barbara.   II. Title.
III. Series.
HG6024.A3A66   2000
332.64'5—dc21   99-56821
                                                                        CIP

PRINTED IN THE UNITED STATES OF AMERICA

9   8   7   6   5   4   3   2   1

TABLE OF CONTENTS

INTRODUCTION

The financial markets have undergone tremendous change in the last twenty years, including the introduction of a variety of financial instruments. None has been more exciting to investors than the expansion and growth of the options and futures markets. Both markets have captured the imagination of investors and dramatically altered the investment arena.

The growth of these markets has stunned even the most optimistic observers. Although the history of options extends back several centuries, it was not until 1973 that standardized, exchange-listed, and government-regulated options became available on the Chicago Board Options Exchange (CBOE). By the early 1980s, the daily volume of trading in stock options had reached the point where the number of shares underlying the options frequently exceeded the daily volume of shares traded on the New York Stock Exchange (NYSE). The bull market of the 1990s caused a surge in options trading. In the period from 1992 to 1998, the number of contracts traded increased by a jolting 400 percent to 400 million contracts. The new world of options trading, once considered too risky for most individuals, is now widely embraced. Although professional investors are still active traders, the current boom is largely the result of heightened trading by individual investors.

A similar pattern exists in the futures market. The trading volume in futures has increased in excess of 20 percent per year for the past twenty-five years. One estimate placed the dollar value of all futures contracts traded in the United States in 1999 at more than $30 trillion! The volume of Treasury bond futures alone is greater than the volume of stocks traded on the New York Stock Exchange.

Options and futures are called *derivative* instruments (see Key 46). The term refers to the fact that the value of these instruments is *derived* from the stocks, bonds, indexes, currencies, and so on, upon which they are based. Price moves in these instruments closely parallel what is occurring in the cash markets, where stocks, bonds, and currencies are traded. In reality, traders in these instruments are also traders in the underlying securities.

Although most investors realize that options and futures are risky and speculative investments, they seldom appreciate their role as risk-management tools. These markets allow speculators to bear risk and hedgers to transfer risk. Hedgers are individuals and firms that make purchases and sales in these markets solely to establish a predetermined price level. Theoretically, the speculator assumes the price risk that the hedger is seeking to minimize. When the hedger sells futures, it is the speculator who buys; alternatively, when the hedger buys futures, it is the speculator who sells. A hedge is simply a transaction designed to minimize an existing or anticipated risk. Originally, the purpose of futures was to transfer risk from one party to another and to smooth out price fluctuations. Subsequently, speculation itself became an important factor in these markets. Speculators play an important role in making the options and futures markets more liquid by making it easier for those who buy and sell these instruments to execute trades.

Investors who wish to speculate in options and futures should be aware of the extreme risk involved. These investments are not for the casual investor. Most speculators in these markets lose money. Only sophisticated and disciplined speculators can expect to make consistent profit. However, the chance of success can be improved significantly by thinking logically, negotiating low execution costs, dealing with an experienced and knowledgeable broker, and setting reasonable goals.

1

OPTIONS

A stock option is a contract that gives to its holder the right, but not the obligation, to buy or sell shares of the underlying security at a specified price on or before a given date. After this date, the option expires. Therefore, options contracts specify three conditions:

1. Property to be delivered
2. Price of the property
3. Specified period during which the right held by the buyer can be exercised

Options have standardized terms, including the exercise (strike) price and the expiration time. This standardization makes it possible for buyers or writers (sellers) of options to close out their positions by offsetting sales and purchases. By selling an option with the same terms as the one purchased, or buying with the same terms as the one sold, an investor can liquidate a position at any time.

Options can be a versatile investment vehicle for investors who understand their risks and limitations. Strategies are not limited to buying, selling, and staying out of the market. Options allow investors to tailor their positions to individual situations and be as conservative or as speculative as they wish. An investor can reap the following benefits from options:

- Protection of stock holdings from a decline in market price
- Increased income against current stock holdings
- Purchase of stock at a lower price
- Benefit to an investor from a big market move without knowing the direction of the move

- Benefit to an investor from the rise or fall of a stock without the cost of actually buying or selling the stock

Since the creation of the Chicago Board Options Exchange (CBOE) in 1973, trading volume in stock options has grown remarkably. The listed option has become a practical investment vehicle for institutions and individuals seeking financial profit or protection. The CBOE is the world's largest options exchange. Options also are traded on the American Stock Exchange (AMEX), the Pacific Exchange (PCX), and the Philadelphia Stock Exchange (PHLX). Options are not limited to common stock. They are written on bonds, currencies, foreign exchanges, specific industries, and various indexes. The CBOE trades options on listed and over-the-counter stocks, on Standard & Poor's 100 and 500 market indexes, Russell 2000 Index, and NASDAQ-100 Index, on U.S. Treasury bonds and notes, on long-term and short-term interest rates, and on the Dow Jones Industrial Average (DJIA). In 1999, the CBOE listed more than 1,200 options on the stock of foreign and domestic companies, 41 index options, 171 equity LEAPS, and 11 index LEAPS (see Key 22).

Options traded on exchanges such as the CBOE are *similar* in many respects to common stocks:

- Options are listed securities.
- Orders to buy and sell options are conducted through brokers in the same manner as orders to buy and sell stock. Similar to common stock, orders on listed options are auctioned on the trading floor of a national exchange.
- Price, volume, and other information about options is instantly available.

The following are some crucial *differences* between common stocks and options:

- There is no fixed number of options. The number of available options depends upon the number of buyers and sellers.
- There are no certificates as evidence of ownership. Printed statements prepared by the involved brokerage firms indicate ownership of options.
- An option is a wasting asset. If it is not sold or exercised before expiration, it becomes worthless and the holder loses the full amount paid for the option.

2

OPTIONS
TERMINOLOGY

The options market has a language all its own. Some of the more important terms include:

- *Options writer.* An options writer is the seller or issuer of an options contract. For example, if the buyer exercises an ABC call option, the options writer must deliver the required number of shares of ABC common stock. The options writer is sometimes called the options seller. A covered option means that the writer owns the underlying security. A naked option occurs when the writer does not own the underlying security.

- *Options buyer or holder.* The options buyer is the investor who obtains the right specified in the options contract. For example, the buyer of an ABC call or put has the right, but not the obligation, to purchase or sell, respectively, shares of ABC Corporation common stock at a specified price within a specified period.

- *Strike (exercise) price.* The price at which the holder can sell to or buy from the writer the item underlying the option. For example, an ABC 50 call option gives the holder the right to purchase 100 shares of ABC stock at a price of $50 per share. On the other hand, an ABC 40 put option gives the holder the right to sell 100 shares of ABC common stock at a price of $40 per share. In index options, settlement is made through the payment of cash rather than the delivery of property.

- *Expiration date.* The expiration date is the last date on which the holder can exercise an option. If an option has not been exercised before expiration, it ceases to exist and is worthless. Options expire on the Saturday following the third Friday of the month in which they can be exercised.
- *Premium.* The premium is the price that the buyer of an option pays and the writer of the option receives. Premiums vary in response to such variables as the relationship between the strike price and the current market value of the underlying security, the volatility of thc underlying security, the amount of time remaining until expiration, the current interest rates, and the effect of supply and demand in the options market. Option premiums are a nonrefundable payment from the options buyer to the options writer for the rights conveyed by the option.
- *Out-of-the-money option.* A call option is out of the money when the strike price is greater than the market price of the underlying interest. A put option is out of the money when the strike price is lower than the market price of the underlying interest. Premiums are lower when options are out of the money.
- *In-the-money options.* A call option is in the money when the strike price is less than the market price of the underlying interest. A put option is in the money when the strike price is greater than the market price of the underlying interest.
- *At-the-money option.* Options are at the money when the common stock price is equal to the strike price.
- *American-style and European-style options.* An American-style option can be exercised by the holder at any time after it is purchased until it expires. A European-style option may be exercised

only on the expiration date. Most exchange-traded stock options are American-style.

- *Straddle.* A straddle is the simultaneous purchase of a put and call on the same stock, with the identical strike price and expiration month (see Key 20).
- *Spread.* A spread is the purchase and sale of options on the same underlying stock (see Key 21).

3

CALL OPTIONS

A call option gives its holder the right to buy a specified number of shares of the underlying stock at a predetermined price (strike price) between the date of purchase and the option's expiration date. It must be emphasized that an option gives an investor the right to purchase, but not the obligation to do so. A single call option gives the holder the right to buy 100 shares. For example, an investor who bought an XYZ October 40 call option would have the right, but not the obligation, to buy 100 shares of XYZ common stock at a cost of $40 per share at any time before the option expires in October. The right to purchase common stock at a fixed price becomes more valuable as the price of the underlying common stock increases.

EXAMPLE:
Suppose an investor buys an XYZ 40 call option when the price of the stock is $40 and pays a premium of $2. A premium or price of $2 means that the option will cost $200 (an option contract is based upon 100 shares). If the price of XYZ stock climbs to $45 before expiration and the premium rises to $6, an investor has two choices in disposing of the option:

1. The option can be exercised and the underlying XYZ common stock can be bought for the total cost of $4,200 ($40 × 100 plus the $200 premium). The shares can then be sold for $4,500, yielding a net profit of $300.
2. The option contract can be sold for $600, earning a profit of $400 ($600 – $200 premium). Here, the

investor makes a profit of 33⅓ percent (200/600), whereas the profit on an outright purchase given the same price would be only 12½ percent [($45 − $40) ÷ $40].

An option does not have to be exercised to lock in a profit. Like common stocks, options are regularly bought and sold on the exchanges. Whether it is more advantageous to exercise or sell a profitable option is influenced by whether an investor desires to own the common stock. In making the decision to exercise the option or to sell the option, the investor must consider premium levels, commissions, and taxes. Unless the investor wants the stock, it is generally better to reap the profit by selling the option itself.

Of course, stock prices often do not move in the direction anticipated or desired. Using the previous example, assume that XYZ common stock fell to $35 and the option premium dropped to ¾ ($75 total). The investor could sell the option to partially offset the $200 premium, and the loss would be $125. If one did not take action, and the option expired worthless, the loss would be the total amount of the premium paid—$200. This loss would be less than if the 100 shares had been purchased outright. An outright purchase would have produced a loss of $500 ($4,000 less $3,500).

The examples illustrate the two main advantages of options:

1. *Leverage.* A somewhat smaller investment controls a larger investment with corresponding greater profit potential.
2. *Limited and defined risk.* Despite how much XYZ stock falls, the maximum risk exposure is limited to the premium. In our example, the maximum loss that could be incurred on this option is the premium of $200.

4

PUT OPTIONS

A put option gives the holder the right to sell a specified number of shares of the underlying common stock at a predetermined price (strike price) on or before the expiration date of the contract. Buying an XYZ October 40 put gives an investor the right to sell 100 shares of XYZ stock at $40 per share at any time before the option expires in October.

EXAMPLE:
Assume that an investor buys an XYZ October 40 put at a premium of $2 (or $200) when the price of the underlying common shares is $40 per share. If the price of XYZ stock falls to $35 before October and the premium rises to $6, there are two choices in disposing of these in-the-money (the strike price is greater than the market price) put options:

1. One hundred shares of XYZ stock can be purchased at $35 per share. Then, the put options can be exercised to sell XYZ at $40 per share. This action produces a profit of $300 ($500 profit on the common stock minus the $200 option premium).
2. The put option contract can be sold, producing a profit of $400 ($600 premium received less the $200 premium paid).

As discussed previously, an option does not have to be exercised to realize profit. It generally is a better strategy to sell an option than to exercise it. Sales of options usually involve lower transactions costs than exercising options.

If XYZ stock had climbed to $45 before expiration and the premium fell to $1, the option would be out of the money. The investor could continue to hold the option, hoping the price will drop, or sell it for $100. A sale for $100 would mean a $100 loss ($200 less $100). It is often a good strategy to sell an option at a loss rather than wait for the price of the stock to change in the investor's favor. The time value of an option rapidly shrinks toward zero, starting about six weeks before expiration.

Short Sales vs. Put Options. An investor who anticipates declining stock prices can purchase put options or sell stock short. A *short sale* is the sale of a common stock that is not owned with the intention of repurchasing it later at a lower price. The investor borrows the stock from another investor through a broker and sells it in the market. Usually, a broker has other clients who own the security and are willing to loan shares.

An important aspect of a short sale order is that an investor does not receive the proceeds of the order at the time the trade is executed. In a short sale, the money is kept by the brokerage firm until the short is covered; that is, until the security is purchased and returned to the lender. Also, to ensure that the short position will be covered, the broker requires the posting of collateral. Most short selling is done through margin accounts, in which case short sellers are required to have in their account the required percentage of the stock's price (currently 50 percent).

The objectives of the put option purchaser are the same as those of the short seller. They are both trying to make a profit from anticipated declines in stock prices. Unlike the short seller, however, the put buyer faces a maximum loss defined by the amount of the premium. A short seller has no limit on the loss that can be sustained. In addition, the short seller faces margin requirements and additional restrictions not applied to the put buyer. On the other hand, the option's limited life span constrains the put buyer. With options, an investor can be correct in anticipating a future price change, but still lose money because the price change did not occur within the limited period of the life of the option.

5

OPTIONS CLEARING CORPORATION

The Options Clearing Corporation (OCC) is the largest clearing organization in the world for options. A clearing organization guarantees that the terms of a contract will be honored, for example, an options contract. In the options market, the OCC provides highly reliable clearance, settlement, and guarantee services. A wholly owned subsidiary, the Intermarket Clearing Corporation (ICC), provides the same benefits to the futures industry. The OCC is regulated by the Securities and Exchange Commission (SEC).

An options buyer looks to the OCC rather than to any particular options writer for settlement. Similarly, the obligations of options writers are owed to the OCC rather than to any particular buyer. In other words, after the OCC is satisfied that there are matching orders from a buyer and a seller and that the premium has been paid, it severs the direct link between the parties and assumes the roles of buyer and seller. Because every option transaction involves both a buyer and a seller, the aggregate rights of options holders are matched by the aggregate obligations that options writers owe to the OCC.

This process benefits both the buyer and seller. The buyer and seller are free to act independently of each other. For example, a seller may buy the same option he/she has written, canceling out the initial transaction and terminating the obligation to deliver the stock. This action does not affect the right of the original buyer to sell, hold, or exercise that option. In addition, the OCC always guarantees all options that it issues.

The OCC was founded in 1973 as a clearing corporation for the Chicago Board Options Exchange (CBOE). The trading success of listed stock options at the CBOE encouraged other exchanges to enter the options marketplace. Currently, the OCC accepts and clears trades for four organizations: (1) the CBOE, (2) the American Stock Exchange (AMEX), (3) the Pacific Exchange (PCX), and (4) the Philadelphia Stock Exchange (PHLX).

In its role as the issuer and guarantor of listed options contracts, the OCC faces certain risks and performance obligations. To ensure the financial integrity of the markets it clears and to protect the interest of its members, the OCC has implemented a comprehensive series of safeguards, including rigorous membership standards, financial surveillance programs, margin requirements, and a clearing fund.

Each clearing member applicant is subject to an initial assessment of its operating capability and creditworthiness. Following receipt of an application and the necessary financial information, an on-site examination of the applicant's records and an operations orientation are conducted by the OCC staff. A recommendation is then submitted to the OCC's board of directors. Final approval for membership requires a majority vote by the board.

The OCC's financial surveillance programs are rigorous and continuous. Its staff members in charge of surveillance routinely:

- Monitor the operational and financial condition of each clearing member
- Monitor general market conditions and the OCC's exposure with respect to specific clearing members on a daily basis
- Evaluate the adequacy of the OCC's margin on a daily basis

The OCC's first line of defense should a clearing member default is the margin deposit base for that member's account. Margin is the amount deposited as collateral for the writers' positions that a clearing member carries. The objective of the OCC's margin system is to accurately measure the OCC's exposure to risk and establish reserves that protect clearing members and the OCC against defaults. Rules established by the Margin Committee of the OCC state that an options seller must deposit either the underlying interest or maintain specified margin in the form of cash, U.S. government securities, bank letters of credit, or other acceptable securities.

The OCC's second line of defense is its members' contributions to the clearing fund. The entire clearing fund is available to cover losses in the event that the margin and clearing fund deposits of the defaulting member are inadequate. The OCC's clearing fund totaled about $1.3 billion at the end of 1998.

6

OPTIONS QUOTES

Major newspapers like *The Wall Street Journal* and *Investor's Business Daily* publish premiums (prices) for exchange-traded options. Exhibit 1 illustrates the information presented in the final market price quotations. Note that there are prices for different months. Exchange-listed options expire on the Saturday following the third Friday of the expiration month.

Originally, all exchange-traded options expired according to one of three standard expiration cycles (with expiration on the Saturday following the third Friday):

1. January/April/July/October
2. February/May/August/November
3. March/June/September/December

This simple expiration cycle, however, was changed by the exchanges because they found that the most actively traded contracts were the ones with the shortest terms. All equity options still have four expiration months. These months are the nearest two plus two additional taken from one of the original standard expiration cycles. Therefore, stocks have options with four different expiration months, even though many newspapers only show the quotes for the closest three months. To illustrate, a stock from the January cycle would have the following trading months available after the January expiration: February, March, April, and July. Because each stock has four expiration months trading simultaneously, an individual stock may have as many as four puts and four calls with the same strike price, but different expiration dates. For example, Merck could trade

February 70s, March 70s, April 70s, and July 70s.

Options can be traded with a common expiration date but different strike prices. For example, in the exhibit, IBM has 105s, 110s, 115s, 120s, 125s, and 130s all expiring in October. The different strike prices are introduced when there is a significant change in the underlying stock price. New strike prices for stock options usually are introduced at 2½-point intervals for stocks trading below 25 to 200, and at 10-point intervals for stocks trading above 200. New listings are added when a stock reaches the high or low strike price.

EXAMPLE:

Stock options with strike prices of $30, $35, and $40 are introduced when the stock is trading at $35 per share. If the stock should drop to $30, new options are introduced with a $25 strike price. If the stock price should thereafter rise to $40, additional options with a strike price of $45 would be introduced. A long list of strike prices indicates that the stock has moved over a wide range over the life of the option.

Premiums are quoted in multiples of ¹⁄₁₆ for options priced below $3, and ⅛ for other options. To a large extent, the premium is the central focus of options trading. Most investors wish to purchase an option when the premium is low and sell the same option at a higher premium. Alternatively, for options writers, the premium received is a source of additional income or a hedge against a possible decline in the price of stocks owned or to be purchased.

EXHIBIT 1
How to Read Options Quotations

Stock price—the closing price for that day on the primary exchange at which the underlying stock is traded.

Option expiration month

Option—the underlying security.

CHICAGO BOARD

Option & Strike NY Close Price			Calls-Last			Puts-Last		
			Aug	Sep	Oct	Aug	Sep	Oct
IBM		105	11	s	12⅞	⅛	s	½
115	⅝	110	6¼	7½	9	⅜	⅞	1⁵⁄₁₆
115	⅝	115	2⅛	3¾	5½	1¹⁵⁄₁₆	2¼	2¾
115	⅝	120	⁹⁄₁₆	⅝	3	⅞	5	5½
115	⅝	125	s	s	1⁷⁄₁₆	s	s	s
115	⅝	130	s	s	⅝	s	s	15¼

r—Not traded. s—No option offered.
Last = premium (purchase price per share)

Strike Price—for calls, the price at which the option buyer may acquire the stock from an option writer; for puts, the price at which the option buyer may sell stock to an option writer.

Last—the option's last sale price (premium per share). Most option contracts are for 100 shares of stock. (Possible contract adjustments resulting in other than 100 shares of stock should be checked in detail with your broker.)

Source: Understanding Options, Chicago Board Options Exchange, Chicago, IL, 1989, p. 12.

7

VALUATION OF CALL OPTIONS

Six factors determine the value of an American-style call option. Recall that an American-style call option may be exercised at any time before the expiration date, whereas a European-style option may be exercised only on the expiration date. Premiums are determined by the relationship to the following factors:

- *Stock price.* The call's price rises when the price of the stock rises, and falls when the price of the stock falls. The relationship is based upon the fact that an option represents a leveraged position in the underlying stock. A relatively small initial premium gains control of a larger asset with significant profit potential. A call option has intrinsic value (the amount by which an option is in the money) if the stock price is greater than the strike price. At a given strike price, the price of the common stock determines whether the option is in the money (stock price > strike price) and therefore has intrinsic value, or out of the money (stock price < strike price) and has only time value (the option's premium above any intrinsic value).
- *Cash dividends.* The value of a call option is inversely related to the dividends paid on the common stock. To illustrate, consider what happens on the ex-dividend date. On this date, stockholders are not eligible to receive the dividend and the market price on the opening sale is reduced by the amount of the dividend. Because the stock's price

declines by the amount of the dividend, the call option price should drop in a corresponding fashion.

- *Stock price volatility.* A positive relationship exists between the volatility of the underlying stock and the value of the call option. The greater the volatility, the greater the potential that the call option will gain intrinsic value and be in the money. In other words, volatile stocks have greater movement, which increases the likelihood that at some time before the option expires, it will be in the money. If the call option is in the money at expiration, it will be profitable for the holder to exercise the option.

- *Time to maturity.* A major determinant of the value of an option is its time to maturity. The longer the period to maturity, the greater the value of the option. The longer the time frame, the greater the chance that options will gain intrinsic value. This relationship is why longer-term call options on a given common stock and exercise price will have higher prices than shorter-term options.

- *Strike price.* The call option price is higher when the strike price is lower, and lower when the strike price is higher. Out-of-the-money call options have lower premiums because they have lower intrinsic values. As call options go in the money, their intrinsic values increase and the premiums rise. For example, consider a common stock trading at $60 per share. A call option with a strike price of $50 has a greater value than a call option with a strike price of $55. The $50 option is in the money by $10, whereas the $55 option is in the money by only $5.

- *Interest rates.* The final factor is the positive relationship between the market interest rate and the value of a call option. Higher interest rates generally produce higher call option prices, whereas lower interest rates result in lower call option prices. In effect, a call option buyer's leveraged position is being financed by a loan from a call option writer. The call option writer defers the benefits of converting the stock to cash by enabling the options buyer to leverage a position in the common stock. Higher interest rates mean that the opportunity cost of entering the agreement with the options buyer is greater for the options seller. Therefore, an options writer will demand a higher call option premium to compensate for the inability to take advantage of the higher interest rates.

Intrinsic Value and Time Value. The value of an option consists of two components: intrinsic value and time value. *Intrinsic value* reflects the amount by which an option is in the money. For example, when the market price of ABC stock is $56 per share, an ABC 50 call option has an intrinsic value of $6. If the underlying stock declines to $52, the intrinsic value of the call option is only $2. However, if the price of the underlying stock drops to $50 or less, the call option lacks intrinsic value.

Time value is the value a call option has in addition to its intrinsic value. The premium reflects what the buyer is willing to pay for an option in anticipation of price increases of the underlying stock before expiration. For example, when the market price of ABC common stock is $50 per share, an ABC 50 call option may command a premium of $2. This premium is entirely time value; it reflects the hope that the underlying security will rise sufficiently to enable the holder to sell or exercise the option. The time value of an option typically decreases as the call option approaches expiration and eventually becomes worthless. Just before the call option's expiration date, its premium is either zero or equal to its intrinsic value. At this point, its time value is zero, and the option price or premium is solely determined by its intrinsic value. The components of the premium may be expressed by the following formula:

Option Premium = Intrinsic Value + Time Value

This formula applies to both put and call options. For in-the-money options, the time value is the amount in excess of intrinsic value. For at-the-money and out-of-the-money options, the time value is equal to the option premium.

8

VALUATION OF PUT OPTIONS

Like all items traded in a competitive economy, the supply and demand for an option determines the price or premium of the option. During periods of rising stock prices, the demand for calls grows stronger and call premiums tend to rise. During periods of declining or stable prices, call premiums tend to be lower. Alternatively, strong stock prices tend to reduce the demand for puts, and put premiums tend to decline, whereas weak stock prices generally increase the demand for puts, exerting upward pressure on put premiums.

Although this analysis provides a general explanation for changes in premiums, more specific factors can be defined that primarily account for the changes in put option prices. The factors are the same as the factors that affect call option prices. They include the following:

- *Stock price.* The value of a put option rises when the price of the stock falls, and falls when the price of the stock rises. At a given strike price, the price of the stock determines whether the option is in the money and has intrinsic value or if it is out of the money and has only time value. Because a put option grants the right to sell shares at the strike price, this right becomes less valuable to the owner as the stock price rises and the put option loses intrinsic value. If the price of the underlying common stock declines, the put option gains intrinsic value.
- *Cash dividends.* The put option's value increases when the underlying common stock pays cash dividends. A stock's price should decline by the

amount of the cash dividend on the ex-dividend date. The ex-dividend date begins the period during which purchasers of the stock cannot receive the next quarterly dividend. That dividend goes to the seller.

- *Stock price volatility.* The final factor is the volatility of the underlying stock price. The more volatile the stock, the higher the price of the put option. The greater the volatility of the stock price, the greater the potential for the option to gain intrinsic value. Volatility is nondirectional in that the fluctuation could be up or down. Consequently, when higher volatility is expected, premiums on both puts and calls rise.

- *Time to maturity.* A significant factor in determining the premium of a put option is the time to maturity. The longer the time to maturity, the greater the value of the option. Longer-term put options command higher premiums. The put option's time value slowly declines until about six weeks before expiration. After that, the dissipation of time value accelerates.

- *Strike (exercise) price.* The value of a put option is greater the higher the strike price, and smaller the lower the strike price. This relationship exists because put options gain intrinsic value as strike prices increase. In other words, for a given stock price, the higher the strike price, the greater the value of a put. For example, assume a stock sells for $50. A put option with a strike price of $60 has a higher value than an option with a strike price of $55. The first put is in the money by $10, whereas the second put is in the money by only $5.

- *Interest rates.* Put option prices rise when interest rates fall, and fall when interest rates rise. One way to explain this relationship is to use the present value argument. The premium on the put option reflects the present value of the strike price. The higher the interest rate, the lower the present value of the strike price and the lower the intrinsic value of the option. Lower intrinsic values translate into lower premiums. Alternatively, lower interest rates increase the present value of the strike price, which increases intrinsic value. A higher intrinsic value results in higher premiums.

9

DELTA

A key concept in options theory is delta. Delta measures the change in an option's price (premium) relative to the change in the underlying price of the stock. Call option deltas are positive and put option deltas are negative because call options have a positive relationship and put options a negative relationship with the underlying stock's price. Call option deltas usually range in value from 0 to 1. A call delta of 0.50 indicates that a 1-point increase in the stock should be accompanied by a ½-point increase in the call premium. For a put with a delta of −0.25, a 1-point increase in the stock should produce a ¼-point drop in the put premium. A higher delta indicates that a call option price will have a greater reaction to a rise or fall in the price of a stock. Conversely, the lower the delta, the more responsive put premiums are to changes in the price of a stock.

At-the-money (price of the stock = exercise price) call and put options have deltas of approximately +½ and −½, respectively. Deep-in-the-money call options (underlying stock is more than 5 points above the strike price) have deltas that approximate +1 and deep-in-the-money put options (underlying stock is more than 5 points below the strike price) have deltas of approximately −1. When option positions are deep out of the money, their deltas approach zero.

EXAMPLE:
The strike price of a call is $40, and the underlying stock is currently priced at $49. This call is deep in the money and its delta should approach 1. The premium should experience a $1 price increase for each $1 gain in the price of the

stock. Premiums for deep-in-the-money options consist almost entirely of intrinsic value and are almost perfect surrogates for positions in the underlying stock.

EXAMPLE:
The strike price of a call is $40, and the underlying stock is currently valued at $40. This call is at the money and its delta should approximate $+\frac{1}{2}$. A 1-point change in the price of the stock should produce a $\frac{1}{2}$-point change in the premium. This option has no intrinsic value currently, but has the potential to gain intrinsic value in the future. The delta value of $+\frac{1}{2}$ reflects this profit potential.

EXAMPLE:
A call has a strike price of $55, and the stock is currently priced at $43. This deep-out-of-the-money option's delta approaches 0. A 1-point movement in the stock will have little or no effect on the premium. Deep-out-of-the-money options have no intrinsic value, extremely small deltas, and little chance of being exercised by the holder.

Investors should assess their risks in options daily. Computing deltas forces investors to confront the risk they are assuming in trading options. Observing an option's premium in relationship to changes in the price of stock often can spotlight distortions in time value (amount by which the premium exceeds intrinsic value).

EXAMPLE:
An investor owns 100 shares of a common stock purchased at $50 per share. Three weeks later, the stock has risen from $50 to $53, following a takeover rumor. The 50 call option rose from 3 to 7, an increase of 4 points. The delta would show a value of 1.33 (4 points $\div$ $3 increase, or $\frac{4}{3}$).

An option's delta can be used in managing risk. The delta tells the investor who owns options the number of shares required to construct a position that will protect the investor from the effects of price movements in the underlying stock. The combination of options and stock to create such a position is called a *delta-neutral.* The total value of the position will remain stable despite changes in the prices of the individual components.

For example, suppose that XYZ's common stock is trading at 41, and the 3-month put options and call options, with exercise prices of 40, have prices of 2 and 4, respectively. Assume that the call option's delta is 0.70. Because the put option is the opposite of the call option, its delta can be computed by subtracting 1 from the call's delta. Therefore, the put option's delta is −0.30 (0.70 − 1.00). These values imply that a $1 increase in the price of the stock will increase the call option's price by $0.70 and reduce the put option's price by $0.30. A delta-neutral call position can be created by purchasing 70 shares of XYZ stock for every call option sold, whereas a delta-neutral put option can be produced by purchasing 30 shares of stock for every put option purchased.

10

COVERED CALL WRITING

Investors use two strategies involving stock options to offset risk: (1) covered call writing and (2) protective puts (Key 12). The strategy of choice for an investor is dependent upon the extent of the expected stock or stock market decline. Many investors view options as highly speculative, risky investments. However, there are several options strategies that are conservative. One such strategy is covered call writing. Investors write covered calls for the following two reasons:

1. Realize additional income on the underlying common stock by earning premium income
2. Provide a measure of downside protection (limited to the amount of the premium) against small declines in the price of the stock

Covered call writing usually is considered to be a more conservative strategy than the outright purchase of common stock, because the investor's downside risk is reduced by the amount of the premium received for selling the call.

The covered call writer either buys common stock and simultaneously sells an equivalent number of call options against the shares purchased (commonly called a "buy-write"), or sells calls against common stock that is already owned. Any investor can profit from this strategy. Its characteristics can be summarized as follows:

- The sale of the option provides immediate cash flow.

- Losses are reduced by the amount of the premium in the event of a downward movement in the price of the common stock.
- It provides a good return even if the underlying common stock is called away (exercised).

A covered call writer owns the underlying common stock but is willing to forgo price increases in excess of the option stock price in return for the premium.

A writer should be prepared to deliver the common stock shares, if assigned, at any time during the life of the option. Assignment is the act of exercise against a seller, which is executed on a random basis or in accordance with procedures established by the Options Clearing Corporation and brokerage firms. To avoid losing the stock, an investor may cancel the obligation at any time by executing a closing transaction. A closing transaction is performed by buying a call in the same series (options with identical terms).

A good strategy is to sell out-of-the-money calls (strike price > current price) with about two months until expiration. The current expiration month should be avoided because option prices decline as they get closer to expiration. Also, far out-of-the-money calls should be avoided because the sale will produce minimal proceeds.

EXAMPLE:

1. Buy 200 shares of XYZ at $28		$5,600
2. Less option premium for 2 April 30 calls (at a premium of $3 per option)		– 600
3. Net investment		$5,000

The gain or loss from possible price movements can be illustrated as follows ($28 = stock purchase price):

I. If the common stock climbs above $30, the investor will not participate in the advance above $30 because the option will be exercised.

II. Maximum profit potential if stock reaches $30:

a. Sell 200 shares at strike price of $30	$6,000
b. Less initial purchase	–5,600
c. Gain from stock sale	400
d. Plus option premium received	600
e. Net profit	$1,000

III. Stock price is unchanged:

a. Stock remains at $28	$5,600
b. Less initial purchase	–5,600
c. Gain in stock price	0
d. Plus option premium received	600
e. Net profit	$600

IV. A price decline to break-even point ($28 – $3 per share premium received = $25):

a. Net investment	$5,000
b. Divide total by number of shares purchased ($5,000/200)	$25

V. If the stock price drops below the break-even point, the investor will suffer a dollar-for-dollar loss below $25. Assume a price decline to $22:

a. Net investment	$5,000
b. Less initial purchase ($3 × 200 shares)	–600
c. Net loss	$5,600

In three of the five possible scenarios, covered writing provides greater profits than outright stock ownership.

11

UNCOVERED CALL WRITING

Uncovered (naked) call writing differs from covered call writing in that the investor does not own the shares of the common stock represented by the option. Further, the potential loss of uncovered call writing is unlimited, whereas covered call writing is a more conservative strategy. An investor who writes an uncovered call option has the objective to earn a return from the writing transaction without investing in the underlying shares of stock. An uncovered call writer must deposit and maintain enough margin (cash and/or securities on deposit) with the broker to guarantee that the stock can be purchased for delivery if the call is exercised.

Writing uncovered calls can be profitable during periods of declining or generally stable prices, but investors who are considering this strategy should be aware of the significant risks involved. If the market price of the underlying common stock sharply increases, the call could be exercised. To satisfy the delivery obligation, the writer would have to acquire stock in the market for substantially more than the strike price of the option. This action could result in a net loss. Therefore, uncovered call writing should be undertaken only by investors who have studied the options market closely and are financially able to afford the risk.

To illustrate, an investor who writes an XYZ October 40 call for a premium of $4 receives $400 ($4 × 100) in premium income. If the stock price remains at or below $40, the calls will not be exercised. However, if the stock price rises to $55 ($1,500 loss), the investor will be assigned and will incur a loss of $1,100 ($1,500 loss on covering the call assignment less the $400 premium). An uncovered call writer may cancel the obligation at any time prior to being assigned by executing a closing purchase transaction (buying a call in the same series). Note that an assignment is the receipt of an exercise notice against a seller that provides an obligation to sell the underlying security at the specified strike price.

12

PROTECTIVE PUTS

A protective put is the simultaneous purchase of a stock and a put option or the purchase of a put related to a stock already owned by the investor. Whereas covered call writing provides a partial hedge against a decline in stock prices, protective puts can provide almost complete protection. If the stock value declines, the price of the put increases, especially when the put is in the money.

A protective put results in unlimited profit potential. The price of protection against loss while retaining the upside potential is the put option's premium. The investor will pay a premium (the cost of the put) to insure against a loss in the stock position. Because the put option is a right to sell at a predetermined price, the purchase of the put predetermines the maximum risk of the stock. This limit on risk occurs because a put entitles the investor to sell the underlying shares at the exercise price of the put at any time through the expiration of the option, despite how much the price of the common stock declines. The investor continues to receive any dividends paid during the period on stock owned. For common stocks that pay substantial dividends, this dividend revenue can substantially reduce the cost of purchasing puts.

The cost of protection can be measured in terms of annualized percent of investment. For example, consider a 6-month XYZ put with a premium of $4 when the stock is trading at $50. The premium of $4 represents 8 percent of the $50 cost of XYZ. Because the 8 percent premium protects the investor for only six months, the annualized cost of protection is 16 percent. The 16 percent annual cost is the price the investor is willing to pay to benefit from any advance in the stock of XYZ while limiting the risk of loss.

The protective put strategy is most effective when the investor feels the price of the stock is vulnerable on the downside. In employing this strategy, the investor probably should stick to the put with a strike price closest to the existing price of the common stock. In addition, it is advisable to purchase a put with at least three months remaining to expiration. This strategy permits the stock sufficient time to make an upward move.

EXAMPLE:

1. Buy 200 shares of XYZ at 40		$8,000
2. Buy two 6-month XYZ 40 puts at 3		+600
3. Net investment		$8,600

The cost of the transaction is $43 ($8,600/200 shares) per share. The purchased put gives the investor the right to sell the shares at $40 at any time up to expiration, no matter what happens to the price of the stock. The premium defines the maximum risk of loss, which in this case is the $3 ($600 in total) price of the put.

The possible price movements and the effect on profits can be illustrated as follows:

I. Maximum gain realized if stock rises above $43 (breakeven). If the price of the stock reaches $50, the put becomes worthless:

a. Sell 200 XYZ at $50	$10,000
b. Less initial purchase price (net investment)	–8,600
c. Net profit on initial investment	$1,400

II. Break-even position:

a. Sell 200 XYZ at $43	$8,600
b. Less initial purchase price	–8,600
c. Net profit	$0

III. Stock price remains unchanged:

a.	Sell 200 XYZ at $40	$8,000
b.	Less initial purchase	−8,600
c.	Net loss on initial purchase = the price of the put	$(600)

IV. The stock declines in price, for example, to $30. The puts can be exercised to sell 200 shares of XYZ at $40 per share. The use of puts limits the loss to the premium paid of $600 rather than the $2,000 loss had the puts not been purchased.

a.	Exercise puts by selling 200 XYZ at $40	$8,000
b.	Less initial purchase price	−8,600
c.	Net loss	$(600)

13

WRITING PUT OPTIONS

The seller (or writer) of a put option is obligated to purchase the underlying stock (normally 100 shares per put option) at the strike price upon receipt of an exercise notice. In return for assuming this risk, the investor is paid a premium at the time the put is written. As a put writer, the investor must be prepared to buy the underlying stock at any time during the life of the option. Investors can write covered or uncovered put options.

Covered Put Writing. A put writer is considered to be *covered* when (a) there exists a corresponding short position or (b) cash deposits or cash equivalents equal to the exercise value of the option are held with a broker. Recall that a short sale is the sale of a security that is not owned with the intention of repurchasing it later at a lower price (Key 4). The investor borrows the stock from another investor through a broker and sells it in the market. Subsequently, the investor repurchases the stock and returns it to the broker. To ensure that the short position is covered, the broker requires the posting of collateral.

A covered put writer's profit potential is limited to the premium received and the difference between the strike price of the put and the original price of the stock shorted. The potential loss of this position is substantial: the price of the stock may increase significantly above the original price of the stock shorted. In this case, the short position will generate losses offset only by the premium received. The covered put writing strategy is not used frequently because uncovered put writing offers the same risk and rewards with generally higher premiums.

Uncovered Put Writing. A put writer is considered to be *uncovered* if (a) there is no corresponding short stock position or (b) no deposits of cash or cash equivalents equal to the exercise value of the put exist. An investor unwilling to purchase stock at the current price might write put options, hoping to acquire the stock at a lower price and, meanwhile, receive premium income. If the put is exercised, the cost of the common stock will be the exercise price less the premium.

EXAMPLE:

The current market price of XYZ is $40 per share. An investor who owns 500 shares would like to acquire 200 more shares at $35 per share. The investor writes two puts with an exercise price of $40 at a premium of $5 per share. The price of the stock drops to $38 per share and the puts are exercised. The investor's cost of acquiring the 200 shares of common stock is $35 per share (the $40 exercise price less the $5 put premium).

In this example, the cost to acquire the shares ($35) is under the current market value of the stock. If the stock declines further, the acquisition price could exceed the market value. This risk explains why this strategy should only be used by sophisticated investors with substantial financial resources.

EXAMPLE:

Suppose the stock in the previous example drops to $20 and the puts are exercised. The put writer's $35 cost of acquiring the stock substantially exceeds the current market value of $20. If the stock in the example increased in price, the puts would not be exercised. The investor would have profit determined by the premium. However, if the stock had advanced $3 to $43 by expiration, the investor could purchase the stock at a net cost of $38 ($43 – $5 premium), which is less than the market price of the stock when the option was written.

14

OPTIONS ON STOCK INDEXES

Stock market indexes were developed to measure performance of the stock market. Most investors gauge the state of the stock market from the news media reports of the Dow Jones averages and the Standard & Poor's (S&P) 500 Index. Index options were introduced in March 1983, when the Chicago Board Options Exchange (CBOE) began trading options on the Standard & Poor's 100 Index (S&P 100). Shortly thereafter, the American Stock Exchange (AMEX) followed with options contracts on the Major Market Index, and the New York Stock Exchange (NYSE) introduced options on the NYSE Composite Index. Within one year of trading, index options accounted for over half of the volume of all options traded. In 1997, Dow Jones and Company gave permission to list options based upon the Dow Jones Industrial Average (DJIA).

S&P 100 Index. The most popular stock index options and the most actively traded of all options is the S&P 100 Index option, which is traded on the CBOE, where 95 percent of the index options and 47 percent of all equity options contracts are traded. The S&P 100 Index is composed of 100 blue-chip stocks on which the CBOE currently lists stock options. Blue-chip stocks are shares of common stock in a nationally known company that has a long history of profit growth and dividend payments. It includes most of the titans of American industry, such as AT&T, Exxon, General Motors, and IBM.

The S&P 100 is a value-weighted index, which means that both the price and number of shares outstanding are used to compute the index. Therefore, stocks with large market capitalizations (market price of the stock times the number of shares outstanding) influence value-weighted indexes most.

To compute the S&P 100 Index, the current market price of each stock in the index is multiplied by the stock's number of outstanding shares. The resulting market values are then added to determine the total market value of the stocks in the index. The current value of the S&P 100 Index is computed by dividing the total market value by the base value and multiplying by 100. The S&P 100 base value initially was determined by the aggregate market value of the 100 stocks as of January 2, 1976. Base values for the S&P 100 Index are adjusted over time to reflect changes in capitalization that result from mergers, acquisitions, splits, and substitutions. The S&P 100 Index is highly correlated with the S&P 500 Index and the DJIA.

Each index options contract has a value of $100 (the index multiplier) times the current value of the index. For example, if the index is at 700, the underlying dollar value of one index options contract equals $70,000 (700 × $100). An index call gives the holder of the option the right, but not the obligation, to buy $100 times the index value at the exercise price. Ownership of an index options contract confers the right to exercise the option. The S&P 100 option is an American-style option, which means that it can be exercised by the holder at any time prior to expiration.

Because the S&P 100 Index is the most widely traded of all index options, an options investor should be aware of its contractual terms. Among the most important terms of the S&P 100 Index options contract are the following:

- *Symbol on the exchange.* OEX.
- *Trading unit.* Each index options contract represents $100 (the index multiplier) times the current value of the S&P 100 Index. For example, when

the index is at 700, the dollar value of a contract will equal $70,000 ($100 × 700).

- *Expiration dates.* S&P 100 Index options expire on a monthly basis in the four nearby months. The final expiration is the Saturday following the third Friday of the expiration month. Investors interested in longer-term options can trade LEAPs (Key 22), which have an expiration of up to three years.
- *Premium quotations.* Options premiums are expressed in terms of dollars and fractions per unit of the index. Each point represents $100. As with stock options, the minimum fraction is $\frac{1}{16}$ for option series trading below 3 and $\frac{1}{8}$ for all other series. For example, a premium of $1\frac{3}{16}$ represents $118.75.
- *Strike prices.* Strike prices are set at 5-point intervals to bracket the current value of the index. New strike prices are added when the current value of the index approaches the limits of the existing strike prices.
- *Aggregate strike prices.* The aggregate strike price is the index multiplier ($100) times the strike price. For example, the aggregate strike price of a 700 option is $70,000 ($100 × 700).
- *Exercise settlement.* Index options are settled by the payment of cash and not by the delivery of the securities that make up the index. Recall that stock options are settled by the delivery of securities. Upon exercise, the options holder receives a cash amount equal to the difference between the closing dollar value of the index on the exercise date and the aggregate strike price of the option.

S&P 500 Index and DJIA. The CBOE also offers S&P 500 Index (SPX) options, which were introduced in 1983. These options are based upon the 500 stocks in the S&P 500 Composite Index. The S&P 500 Index is the most widely followed barometer of stock market movements after the DJIA. It is made up of 400 industrial, 20 transportation, 40 utility, and 40 financial stocks. The index consists primarily of NYSE-listed companies, but also includes some AMEX and NASDAQ stocks. Like the S&P 100 Index, it is a value-weighted series. However, options based on this series differ from S&P 100 Index options in that the S&P 500 Index options are European-style options, which can be exercised only at expiration.

The third major type of index option is based on the DJIA (DJX), a price-weighted index of 30 blue-chip stocks that are listed on the NYSE. "Price-weighted" means that the component stock prices are added together and the result is divided by another figure, the divisor. As a result, a high-priced stock has a greater effect on the index than a low-priced stock. These options quickly received acceptance in the marketplace and are popular with individual investors (Key 15).

15

OPTIONS ON THE DJIA

The Dow Jones Industrial Average (DJIA) is the most widely watched and quoted measure of U.S. stock prices. Over the last century, investors worldwide have discussed the ups and downs in the market by referring to the DJIA. Developed by Charles Dow in 1896, it remains a convenient benchmark for comparing the performance of individual stocks to the course of the market.

The DJIA is composed of 30 "blue-chip" stocks, which represent approximately 20 percent of the $15 trillion market capitalization (price per share times number of shares outstanding) of all U.S. stocks. These stocks are among the most widely held and actively traded on the New York Stock Exchange.

In the past, Dow Jones and Company refused to license the use of its indexes for trading in options and futures. This policy was reversed in 1997 when Dow Jones agreed to allow options based upon the DJIA (symbol is DJX) to be traded exclusively at CBOE. Although both the S&P 100 Index (OEX) and S&P 500 Index (SPX) continue as the pacesetters in index contracts traded, DJX options have been well received by individual investors.

LEAPS. An interesting strategy using DJX options involves the use of LEAPS (Long-term Equity Anticipation Securities). LEAPS (see Key 22) are long-term options with an expiration date as far as three years in the future that allow investors to establish long or short positions. The longer time period until expiration has a significant effect on time decay. The longer exercise term means that the premium is less affected by the passage of time until the option converts into a shorter-term option and is increasingly impacted by time decay. A general rule is that an option's premium declines by 75 percent in the last three weeks of its life.

With LEAPS based upon the DJIA, investors may take a long-term position in all 30 stocks with known risk at a fraction of the cost of purchasing the individual shares. Because the investment time frame of LEAPS is much longer than that of standard DJX options, investors are less concerned with precisely timing the market than with correctly predicting the market trend over time. As with all options transactions, the buyer's risk is limited to the amount of the premium paid.

Strategy. Assume the DJIA is currently at 11,000. Unlike the 20+ percent gains in recent years, an investor expects a more normal return for the upcoming year with only mild volatility along the way. That same investor forecasts that the DJIA will gain about 10 percent over the next year.

An interesting strategy to consider for capitalizing on that forecast is what is called a "bull spread." A spread is the purchase and sale of options on the same underlying stock but with a different expiration date and/or a different strike price (Key 21). In a bull spread, a call is bought at one strike price and a call is sold at a higher strike price (both calls typically expire at the same time). A bear spread is used when an investor is pessimistic about the market and involves the purchase of a put at a higher strike price while selling a put at a lower strike price as a hedge.

DJX is based upon 1/100th of the DJIA, so each point represents $100. For example, when the DJIA is at 11,000, the DJX will trade at 110.00. Several factors affect the overall level of DJX options prices: the underlying index value, the option's strike price, time until expiration, volatility, interest rates, and dividends. The prices of DJX calls and puts prior to expiration reflect both intrinsic value and time value. The most important consideration is the index value compared to the strike price of the option. This relationship determines whether the option is in the money or out of the money. A call or put that is in the money has intrinsic value, which is the amount the holders would receive upon exercise. The intrinsic value of a 110.00 strike DJX call is $3.00 if the DJIA is at 11,300 ($113.00 − 110.00 = $3.00). Similarly, the intrinsic value of a 110.00 strike DJX put is $4.00 if the DJIA falls to 10,600 ($110.00 − 106.00 = $4.00).

The time value of the option consists of the traded price less the intrinsic value. If a 110.00 strike DJX call is trading at $4 with the DJX at 113.00, then its intrinsic value is 3.00 ($113.00 − 110.00 = $3.00), and its time value is $1 ($4 − 3 = $1). Out-of-the-money options have no intrinsic value and, thus, their premiums reflect pure time value.

Forecasting a moderate (10 percent) increase in the DJIA, assume an investor buys both an at-the-money LEAPS call and sells a higher strike LEAPS call with the same expiration date. Because the expectation is for a higher price, this strategy is called a bull spread. A bull spread allows an investor to participate in a forecasted market gain while limiting losses.

Assume a 1-year 110.00 LEAPS call is trading at 10, and five contracts are bought for $5,000 (10 × 5 × $100). A 1-year 132.00 strike LEAPS call (20 percent out of the money) is trading at 4½. If all five contracts are simultaneously sold, the proceeds are $2,250 (4.5 × 5 × $100 = $2,250). The net outlay at the beginning of this strategy is $2,750 ($5,000 − 2,250 = $2,750).

Scenario I: The DJIA rises by 10 percent. The forecast was correct. The DJIA rose from 11,000 to 12,100 (DJX = 121.00) at expiration. The long call position is exercised for a profit of $500 [(121.00 − 110.00 − 10) × 5 × $100 = $500]. Because the DJIA closed below the strike price on the call that is sold short, the profit is the $500 on the long call plus the $2,250 premium retained from the sale of the short call, which totals $2,750.

Scenario II: The DJIA rises by 25 percent. The

43

investor underestimated the strength of the DJIA as it rose from 11,000 to 13,750 (DJX = 137.50) at expiration. The long call position produces a profit of $8,750 [(137.50 − 110 − 10) × 5 × $100 = $8,750]. Because the DJIA rose above the strike price on the short call, the short call position is a loss of $500 [(132 − 137.50 + 4.50) × 5 × $100 = −$500]. The profit on the combined position is $8,250. An important point in this example is that the $8,250 gain is the maximum potential profit that could be made on this position. The sale of the out-of-the-money LEAPS call established a cap on profit potential. For this reason, this strategy is most useful in periods of moderately rising markets.

Scenario III. The DJIA remains at or below 11,000. If the DJIA remains at or below 11,000 at expiration, the entire amount of the investment ($2,750) is lost. This amount is the maximum possible loss on the combined position.

16

USING INDEX OPTIONS

Let's consider some basic options strategies an investor might employ. Assume that an investor anticipates a rise in the market and decides to buy call options to profit from the market's appreciation.

EXAMPLE:
Suppose that on July 1, the S&P 100 Index closed at 670. An investor who buys three September 675 call options at a premium of $12 pays $3,600 (each point on the index represents $100). The market rallies by August with the index standing at 685, and the investor decides to sell at a premium of $15. The investor's profit would be $900.

Selling price of $15 × 3 calls × $100	$4,500
Buying price of $12 × 3 calls × $100	− 3,600
Profit	$900

The investor makes a return of 25 percent ($900/$3,600) on a $3,600 investment. Meanwhile, the index rose from 670 to 685, which represents a 2.2 percent increase. If the index had decreased in value, the maximum loss would be the premium of $3,600 because the maximum loss of any option purchase always is defined by the premiums paid.

As mentioned previously, stock index options are effective tools for hedging strategies. Suppose that an investor of a well-diversified portfolio concludes that the market is about to have a short-term drop. A portfolio that is well diversified is largely insulated from firm-specific and industry risk. However, market risk cannot be diversified away. Several strategies can be used to hedge against this risk. For example, an investor could choose to sell calls. The sale of calls would hedge market risk to the extent of the premiums received from writing the options. The premium could offset some of the downside risk from a general market decline. The risk is the possibility that the index may increase beyond the sum of the exercise price and the premium. In that case, the loss on the options position could exceed the gains on the portfolio.

Another way an investor can hedge a diversified portfolio is to buy index puts. If the market declines, the decrease in the portfolio's value would be at least partially offset by an increase in the value of the puts. The maximum possible loss on this trade would be the premium on the puts.

An investor can provide a portfolio approximate coverage by dividing the portfolio value by the current index times $100 (index multiplier). This value is the number of contracts that equates to the stock portfolio. For a portfolio of $700,000, when the S&P 100 Index is 700, 10 contracts [$700,000 $\div$ (700 $\times$ $100)] would provide approximate coverage. This number may not be a totally accurate hedge because the stock portfolio can change in value to a different extent than the S&P 100 Index.

In a declining market, the puts will produce profits to offset the losses on the stock portfolio. If the market rises, the options position will show losses offsetting appreciation in the stock portfolio. The hedged position should be generally stable in value until the hedge is liquidated.

17

OPTIONS ON INTEREST RATES

Few factors affect stocks, mutual funds, real estate, and fixed-income instruments more than interest rates. Interest rates are a constant topic of discussion in the financial media. The most closely watched interest rates are the rates on Treasury bills, notes, and bonds. Treasury bills, the recognized benchmark of short-term notes, mature in one year or less. Treasury notes mature in two to ten years, whereas Treasury bonds mature and repay their face value 30 years from the date of issue.

Although options on Treasury securities are available, it is also possible to speculate directly on interest rates. No investor should underestimate the difficulty in predicting trends in interest rates. Interest rates reflect changes in the economy, inflationary expectations, and the value of the U.S. dollar. Even economists seldom agree on the future course of interest rates.

The Chicago Board Options Exchange (CBOE) has issued four types of options on interest rates:

1. An option based upon the current rate of the most recently auctioned 13-week Treasury bill (IRX)
2. An option based upon the yield-to-maturity on the most recently auctioned 5-year Treasury note (FVX)
3. An option based upon the 10-year Treasury note (TNX)
4. An option based upon the 30-year Treasury bond (TYX)

All of these options are based upon an underlying

47

value (called a composite) that is calculated using interest rates rather than the price of Treasury bonds or bills. When interest rates rise, the value of the underlying call options tends to rise, whereas a decline in interest rates increases the value of the underlying put option.

The values of all of the composites are 10 times the underlying Treasury rates. For example, an annualized yield of 5 percent on newly auctioned 13-week Treasury bills would place the composite at 50.00. An average yield-to-maturity on the underlying 30-year Treasury bonds of 6 percent would place the composite at 60.00. The values of the composites change as Treasury rates change. For example, if the Treasury bill composite stood at 50.00 and short-term rates rose to 5.5 percent, the Treasury bill composite value would increase to 55.00. For every percentage-point change in interest rates, the interest rate composites change 10 points. All of these options trade on an exchange regulated by the Securities and Exchange Commission. As with other exchange-listed options, investors can buy or sell both puts and calls. Like all listed options, these options offer public bid/ask prices, last-sale information, and an exchange floor with traders obligated to make markets.

18

RISK

Listed stock options have the proven ability to help investors control the risks and rewards of investing in individual common stocks. But what is missing with listed stock options for many investors is the ability to fully hedge against the risk or profit from movements in the overall market. Although individual stocks are affected by movements in the overall market, some stocks tend to be less volatile than the market as a whole, whereas others exceed the volatility of the overall market, and some even move in a direction that is contrary to the market.

Stock index options were designed to fill the need that stock options could not fully satisfy. They enable investors who have opinions about movements in the overall market to hedge against market risk or to profit from movements in the market. Stock index options are, by far, the most actively traded options (Keys 14 and 17). One way to examine risk is to divide it into three components:

1. Market risk
2. Industry risk
3. Firm-specific risk

Market risk (also called *systematic risk*) is the risk that results from movements in the overall market. Market risk affects every stock to some extent. It results from economic factors such as changes in interest rates, inflationary expectations, global investment flows, and consumption spending. Studies have shown that the market component of individual stock risk can be as high as 50 percent.

Industry risk is caused by developments unique to the

industry in which a firm operates. Examples of industry risk include domestic or foreign competition, changes in the regulatory environment in which the industry operates, and product obsolescence. Industry risk tends to be less of a factor in overall risk then market risk.

Firm-specific risk results from factors specific to an individual company. Examples include the departure of key management personnel, strikes, ability to maintain quality, and the development of new products.

Diversification can substantially reduce industry risk and firm-specific risk in an investment portfolio. Diversification is the spreading of risk by allocating funds to a variety of investments. However, diversification cannot significantly reduce market risk. All stock prices move more or less in tandem with the general market. A substantial portion of stock price volatility and nearly all of the risk associated with a well-diversified portfolio is market risk.

19

THE 90/10 STRATEGY

The 90/10 strategy involves purchasing calls on the same number of shares of stock that would have been purchased outright, then investing the difference in a fixed-income security such as Treasury bills. The name of the strategy is derived from the most common proportion in which the assets are allocated: 90 percent in Treasury bills and 10 percent in index call options. This strategy is particularly appropriate for an investor who is not interested in individual stock selection and who wishes to participate in the growth of the stock market with limited risk exposure. Interest on the Treasury bills covers part of the possible loss on the calls. This strategy permits the investor to benefit from a favorable stock price move while limiting the downside risk to the call premium less any interest earned. It is a particularly effective approach in periods of high interest rates because of greater interest income.

EXAMPLE:
Assume that the common stock of XYZ sells at $40 per share. The purchase of 100 shares costs $4,000. The $4,000 represents the maximum amount that can be invested. The alternative would be to use the 90/10 strategy. An index call option would be purchased with a strike price of $40 per share. If the premium is $4 per share, the cost of the option would be $400. This approach leaves the investor with $3,600 that can be invested in Treasury bills.

Suppose the Treasury bills mature in six months and earn 6 percent interest. The $3,600 would earn interest of $108 ($3,600 × .06 × 6/12). This interest reduces the investor's cost of the call to $292 ($400 minus $108). The $292 also represents the investor's maximum risk exposure compared to the $4,000 cost if the 100 shares were purchased outright.

The beauty of this strategy is that although the risk is limited, the potential capital appreciation is not. Once the market price of XYZ increases beyond the strike price, the call buyer could realize the same dollar appreciation at expiration as that of an investor who owns 100 shares of the common stock. Therefore, this strategy limits risk to the net cost of the call while still enabling investors to realize capital appreciation.

20

STRADDLES

A straddle is the simultaneous purchase of a put and a call on the same stock, with the identical strike price and expiration month. Typically, the buyer of a straddle anticipates a substantial movement in a stock but is uncertain what the direction will be. Because the investor is betting on an extraordinary stock movement, the odds of losing are good. Hence, this strategy is risky and should be undertaken only by experienced options traders.

The buyer of a straddle risks losing only the amount of the premium. The maximum loss occurs only if the price of the stock on the expiration date of the options is exactly equal to the strike price. Although it is difficult to lose the entire premium paid for a straddle, it also can be difficult to make a profit. Either the put or the call side of a straddle is almost certain to expire worthless. As a result, the stock has to move substantially for a profit to be made.

EXAMPLE:

Suppose that an investor purchases both a put and a call on a stock, paying $5 for the call and $4 for the put, for a total of $9. Also suppose that the underlying stock's price is $60 and that the strike price of the options is $60. If the price of the stock rises above $69 or drops below $51, the investor will make a profit. Only if the stock expires at the strike price of $60 will the investor lose the entire investment. The investor loses only part of the investment at any other price between $51 and $69.

The investor earns a profit if the stock sells at a price exceeding $69 or drops to less than $51. If the stock rises to $75 and the investor exercises the call at $60, the investor's profit is $6 ($15 minus $9 premium). Alternatively, if the stock drops to $43 per share and the investor exercises his/her put at $60, the profit is $8 ($17 minus $9 premium). Thus, the investor is assured of a profit only if the stock moves by more than $9 in either direction.

One of the most profitable strategies options traders can undertake is straddle writing. This option maneuver involves the issuance of both a put and a call on the same underlying stock when the exercise price and the expiration dates of the put and the call are identical. Conservative investors who write straddles use a covered writing strategy. In other words, straddles are backed by stock ownership in the event the call portion of the straddle is exercised. In addition, they have sufficient funds to pay for any shares they could be forced to buy as a result of the puts being exercised.

In a flat or unchanging market, time works against the straddle buyer and in favor of the straddle writer. The straddle writer's profits rise as maturity approaches because of the decay in time value. The significant weakness of covered straddle writing is that the price of the stock may decline sharply. Every dollar that the stock declines below the strike price reduces the value of the investor's position by one dollar on the stock owned and one dollar on the stock that will be sold by the owner of the put side of the straddle. Using this example, the writer of the straddle will earn a profit as long as the price of the stock involved stays between $51 and $69.

21

SPREADS

A spread is the purchase and sale of options on the same underlying stock. The options may be either at the same exercise price with different expiration months, or at different exercise prices with the same or different expiration months. This sophisticated strategy is aimed at reducing the risk associated with a simple long (opening buy) or short (opening sale) transaction, and should be used only by experienced traders.

There are two basic types of spreads: (1) bull and (2) bear. A *bull spread* involves the purchase of an option with a lower strike price, and the concurrent sale of an option with a higher strike price. In a *bear spread*, the option with a lower strike price is sold, and the option with a higher strike price is bought. A bull spread is most profitable when the underlying stock's value increases, whereas a bear spread is most profitable when the underlying stock's value falls. The simplest way to execute a bull spread is to purchase an at-the-money call option and sell an out-of-the-money call option; both options have the same time to maturity but different exercise prices. The lower-priced option is purchased in the hope that the underlying stock will increase in value between the time of purchase and expiration. If that happens, the long-in-the-money option will increase in value at a faster rate than the higher, short position. For an investor who is confident that the market is going to rise substantially, purchasing calls would be a better strategy. However, a bull spread is less risky than a simple long position because the cost of the long position is reduced by the amount received from the sale of the call option.

EXAMPLE:

A trader buys one October 40 XYZ call and sells one October 45 XYZ call when the underlying stock is priced at $39. If the stock rises to $44, the October 40 call will rise point for point with the underlying stock because it is in the money. The call sold will not increase in value to the same extent because it is still out of the money. The trader could close this position at a profit.

A trader who wants to profit from a declining market and limit risk exposure can engage in a bear spread. The simplest way to accomplish a bear spread is to purchase an at-the-money put option and sell an out-of-the-money put option. In a bear spread, both put options have the same time to maturity but different exercise prices.

EXAMPLE:

A trader buys one October 40 XYZ put and sells one October 35 XYZ put when the underlying stock is $41 per share. If the stock drops to $37, the October 40 put purchased will rise point for point with the drop on the underlying stock, because it is in the money. The put sold will not increase in value to the same extent, because it is still out of the money. The trader could close this portion at a profit.

22

LEAPS

Introduced in 1990, Long-term Equity Anticipation Securities (LEAPS) are options on individual stocks that provide the owner the right to purchase or sell shares of a stock at a specified price on or before a given date up to three years in the future. In contrast, short-term options have an expiration time of up to nine months. Since their introduction, LEAPS have grown rapidly in popularity, particularly among individual investors. In 1999, the Chicago Board Options Exchange (CBOE) estimated that more than half of all outstanding LEAPS were options contracts held by individual investors.

LEAPS trading at CBOE increased nearly 37 percent in 1998. CBOE responded to the growing number of investors who use LEAPS as a stock surrogate by listing 47 new equity LEAPS and two new index LEAPS in 1998. CBOE now lists a total of 171 equity LEAPS and 11 index LEAPS. Currently, four U.S. exchanges trade these options: the Chicago Board Options Exchange (CBOE), the American Stock Exchange (AMEX), the Philadelphia Stock Exchange (PHLX), and the Pacific Exchange (PCX).

LEAPS are available in two types: (1) calls and (2) puts. A call gives its holder the right to buy an underlying number of shares, whereas a put gives its holder the right to sell a set number of shares. The owner of a call has the right during the three-year period, but not the obligation, to purchase the underlying interest, although sellers are obligated to make this sale should the buyer exercise this right. The owner of a put is not obligated to make the sale, although sellers are obligated to buy the underlying interest should the owner exercise the option.

LEAPS options can be effective vehicles for hedging or speculating. LEAPS calls provide those investors with a longer-term view of the stock market an opportunity to benefit from increases in the prices of stocks at a substantially lower price than required to purchase stock. Should a stock appreciate over the three-year term to a level above the exercise price of the LEAPS, an investor could sell the LEAPS contract in the open market for a profit providing the sale price including commissions exceeds the total price paid. As with any option, LEAPS may expire worthless and may fluctuate more than the price of the underlying stock.

LEAPS also can be used to reduce the downside risk of a stock investment. The purchase of a LEAPS put gives the holder the right to sell the underlying stock at the strike price for the life of the option. Index LEAPS options can be effectively used by investors who would like to hedge several stocks in a given industry segment (or even their entire portfolio).

LEAPS vs. Short-term Options. The cost of a typical LEAPS is higher than the cost of a short-term option. However, the higher LEAPS cost is offset by the longer time to expiration. The Pfizer January 2000 LEAPS call option price at the close of July 2, 1999 for a strike price of $40 was $4.50, whereas a short-term options expiring in August 1999 was $1.50 for the same strike price. Pfizer was selling for 38⅝ on July 2, 1999. The LEAPS price was 3 times higher than the short-term option, but the time to expiration for the LEAPS option is 4.1 times greater than the short-term option. On a daily basis, the LEAPS call costs 2.2 cents per share, whereas a short-term option costs 3.0 cents per share (see Exhibit 2).

Although LEAPS always will trade at a higher price than an identical short-term option, the important advantage for LEAPS is that the time value of a new LEAPS is considerably less sensitive to the daily changes in the time to expiration than is a new short-term option. Thus, a LEAPS investor loses less time value for each day the option is held than a short-term option holder. This price advantage applies to both calls and puts. Once a LEAPS option's time to expiration is similar to a short-term option, its price pattern will duplicate that of a short-term option as it moves toward expiration.

Index LEAPS. Many investors use options based upon their belief in movements of the market as a whole rather than anticipating individual stock price movements. Index LEAPS give the investor the ability to create a long-term position in an option that has the same investment horizon as the investor's market position. There are more than forty different index LEAPS ranging from the S&P 500 and S&P 100 to market indexes like those of Mexico and Japan.

S&P Index LEAPS are based upon one-tenth the value of the S&P 500 (SPX) or one-fifth of the value of the S&P 100 (OEX). The Index LEAPS provide the investor with the ability to control market exposure in finer increments because they represent options with considerably smaller underlying values than full-size, shorter-term index options. If OEX is at 700.00, representing an underlying value of $70,000 (700.00 × $100), the OEX LEAPS would be based upon a price of 140.00, representing an underlying value of $14,000 (140.00 × $100).

Contract Dates. Unlike shorter-term options, all LEAPS options expire in January. Short-term options are assigned to one of three cycles:

Cycle	Expiration Months
January	April, July, October
February	May, August, November
March	June, September, December

At any point in time, a short-term option will have contracts with four expiration dates outstanding, the two near-term months and two further-term months. Expiration for both LEAPS and short-term options occurs on the Saturday following the third Friday of the expiration month. Further information on LEAPS can be obtained by contacting the CBOE by phone (800-OPTIONS) or at its Web site (www.cboe.com).

EXHIBIT 2
Time-Value Cost of Pfizer LEAPS vs. Pfizer Short-term Options[*]

Option Type	Strike Price ($)	Premium ($)	No. of Days to Expiration	Cost per Day/per Share (¢)
LEAPS Call	40	4.50	204	2.2
Short-term Call	40	1.50	50	3.0

[*]Pfizer common stock was selling for $38⅜ as of the close on July 2, 1999.

23

VOLATILITY AND THE PUT/CALL RATIO

Option participants have spent millions of dollars and thousands of hours to develop a trading system to assist with the prediction of future options prices. No single indicator will provide the solution to this cternal puzzle. However, it is helpful to track two of the most widely used measures of market sentiment: (1) volatility and (2) the put/call ratio.

Volatility. Volatility is a key element in pricing an option and reflects the chance that a stock, or the market as a whole, will move. Calculating a stock's volatility provides clues as to how likely, and of what magnitude, an option's price will change. Generally, the greater the stock's volatility, the more expensive the option. The higher price reflects the greater probability that the option will expire in the money. Option volatility is expressed as a percentage: a 20 percent volatility suggests that the price could be 20 percent higher or lower from the current level within a year.

Volatility is defined as the annualized standard deviation of percentage moves of a *stock price*. The basic statistical formula is as follows:

$$\sqrt{\frac{\Sigma\,(x - \overline{x})^2}{N}}$$

where
x is the percentage move of each item from day to day
$\overline{x}$ is the average of the series
N is the total number of items in the series

There are numerous adjustments that can be added to make the formula significantly more precise. However, those refinements are beyond the scope of this book. The value calculated using this formula reflects the historical volatility of the stock. Traders are primarily concerned with not what has happened, but rather what will happen. As a result, they measure what the market believes volatility will be in the future, which is called "implied volatility."

The calculation of implied volatility is conceptually very simple. The price of an option is a function of the stock price, strike price, interest rate, time to expiration, and volatility. Because the option price, stock price, strike price, interest rate, and time to expiration are all known, the only unknown variable is volatility. It is referred to as "implied" because it is not known.

The actual calculation involves an interactive process that is time-consuming. Most options software provides this value for an option or a list of options. The CBOE Web site lists recommended software. On the same Web site, historical volatilities for individual options are available by clicking on "Trader's Tools" and then selecting "Historical Volatilities."

The most widely referenced volatility measure is based upon the overall market, called the Market Volatility Index (VIX). This index is a measure of implied volatility of OEX options. It is computed as the volatility of the following:

- Four OEX contracts in two nearby months
- One call and one put just out of the money
- One call and one put just in the money, for each of the two front months

Implied volatility is the expected trading range of the OEX. The VIX is calculated each trading day by the CBOE and is presented on its home page.

Market volatility is a critical factor in determining option premium levels, and volatility normally increases in periods of market distress. The higher the VIX's volatility, the greater the likelihood the market has reached a short-term bottom. A very low implied volatility usually precedes a sharp move in the market. This move is often, but not always, to the downside. These are rough guidelines and not precise forecasting tools. The VIX traditionally ranges from 17 to 25, although in the period from July 1, 1998 to June 30, 1999, its range was from 16.73 to 60.63. *The Wall Street Journal* often discusses volatility in its options report section.

Speculators should be aware that stock price volatility is the only factor determining premiums (prices) that is not directly observable. Because the option price is so dependent upon the change in the stock's volatility, accurate volatility measures are crucial in determining if options are mispriced. Many traders feel that volatility is the most critical element of understanding and profiting from options trading.

Put/Call Ratio. The put/call ratio is the ratio of the volume of put options to the volume of call options. There are two put/call ratios: (1) the index put/call ratio and (2) the equity put/call ratio. The index put/call ratio is based on the OEX option (the most actively traded), option, whereas the equity ratio is based upon the volume of all stock options.

Investors rely on these ratios as contrary sentiment indicators. When too many investors are bullish (buying too many calls), then contrarians are bearish because they believe the majority usually is wrong. Similarly, when too many investors are bearish (buying too many puts), then a contrarian expects the market to climb.

Put/call ratios are not good indicators for many individual stocks because of the distorting effects of takeover rumors and other potential insider information that can stimulate call buying. This weakness is even more compelling for smaller, less-active stocks. However, the put/call ratio has predictive value for very large, liquid stocks that are not subject to takeover rumors. The interpretation of put/call ratios is anything but precise. These ratios should be treated as rough guidelines rather than precise forecasting tools. In addition, these ratios, over time, have exhibited different tendencies as investing patterns have evolved.

Many technical analysts support the use of different moving averages of the ratios as better forecasting tools. Lawrence McMillan in *McMillan on Options* (John Wiley & Sons, 1996) prefers to use both a 21-day moving average and a 55-day moving average of the ratios. He finds the 21-day average to be useful in catching short-term moves, whereas the 55-day average identifies more intermediate-term trends. A 21-day moving average, for example, is determined by adding the options closing price to the closing prices of the previous 20 days and then dividing by 21. The advantage of a moving average is that it can smooth out the bumps and jiggles, revealing the market's true trend.

The CBOE reports the values for puts and calls at the end of the trading day for both equities and indexes. Analysts use one decision rule for equities and another for indexes:

	Equities	Indexes
Bullish	> .75	> 1.5
Neutral	.40–.75	.75–1.5
Bearish	< .40	< .75

Thus, options prices reflect the volatility of the underlying stock prices.

24

TIPS ON BUYING OPTIONS

Options are an exciting part of the investment arena and continue to attract much interest. In 1998, more than 400 million contracts were traded, a 15 percent increase over 1997 and double the number traded in 1992. It's easy to see why options are so attractive to investors. The returns can be many times the option's cost if the buyer anticipates the market correctly. Although buyers may win big, they do not win often. Two conditions make it difficult to generate profit consistently:

1. Options lose value as the expiration date approaches.
2. About a third of all options expire worthless.

With options, investors not only have to be right, but right within a limited time frame. Studies have shown that most of the moneymakers in options are those who sell (write) them. Although the returns on writing calls are not extraordinary, they are consistent. An options investor who adopts a consistent, disciplined strategy and follows some basic rules can earn profits. These basic rules include:

1. *Make it simple.* Do not adopt complicated strategies that are too difficult to understand. Focus upon a few of the more widely used strategies.
2. *Be safe.* Never risk more than can be afforded. Do not exclusively buy short-term calls or puts, betting on explosive moves up or down. The tactic will sooner or later lose money. Options can be a prudent choice to enhance returns when a strategy such as using "covered calls" is adopted.

3. *Choose a reasonable expiration period.* As a rule, options with more than six months to expiration should be avoided. They are more expensive and not as liquid due to the low trading activity. Options that expire in a few weeks also should be avoided. The time value of an option declines very little in the early days of its life, but rapidly shrinks toward zero in the last six weeks before expiration. In fact, the general rule on premium decay is that 75 percent of the premium will evaporate in the last three weeks of an option's life span. Therefore, when buying options, buy time.

4. *Avoid options that have too much or too little intrinsic value.* In-the-money options have intrinsic value and sell for a relatively higher premium. Out-of-the-money options have no intrinsic value and, therefore, sell for a lower premium. Investors should avoid deep-in-the-money options, which are expensive and have limited profit potential. Alternatively, although deep-out-of-the-money options may be tempting because the premiums are so low, only an extraordinary move can make these options profitable. Generally speaking, investors should confine themselves to slightly out-of-the-money, slightly in-the-money, or at-the-money options.

5. *Diversification is absolutely necessary.* Options investors should have at least three options positions on different stocks or indexes. Do not concentrate exclusively on calls, as do many investors who have a bullish orientation. Puts can be used to hedge a portfolio that consists of stocks and/or call options. An appropriate hedge would be between a third and a half of portfolio value.

6. *A partial writing strategy against existing stock positions is an excellent defensive strategy.* An investor with 1,000 shares of stock should sell 4 to 6 calls against the position. This strategy provides

cash flow and downside protection while maintaining upward potential.
7. *Do not sell uncovered (naked) options.* The risk of an options buyer is limited to the premium. Options sellers (writers) who do not have a position in the underlying stock face unlimited risk. The premium received does not justify this risk.
8. *Have a plan.* Select a target price for the option at the time an options position is established and do not deviate from it. Remember that sell orders can be entered at the target price in advance. Also, investors should sell anytime the investment doubles.

25

SELECTING A BROKER

Options can be traded only through a registered broker or dealer. Although brokers and dealers are closely regulated by the Securities and Exchange Commission (SEC), it is important to be careful in selecting one. A broker should be both knowledgeable about the market and effective in meeting the needs of its clients. This knowledge includes all of the following:

- Handling purchase and sale orders
- Offering appropriate advice and research material about options
- Monitoring accounts to ensure there are no clerical errors
- Seeing that money owed to customers is promptly mailed

Before 1995, there were three main types of brokers: (1) full-service, (2) discount, and (3) deep-discount.

Full-service brokers provide recommendations and offer advice to their clients. Most of these brokers are members of firms that have research departments. Some of the largest ones are Merrill Lynch, Prudential Securities, Morgan Stanley Dean Witter, PaineWebber, and Shearson Lehman.

Discount brokers appeal to investors who do their own research, know precisely what they want, and can make their own buy-and-sell decisions. Investors can save between 30 and 70 percent on their commissions by using a discount broker. Discount brokers simply execute orders, employing salaried order clerks who do not receive commissions. They also provide routine services. Examples of discount brokers are Charles Schwab,

Quick & Reilly, and Muriel Sielbert.

Deep-discount brokers charge investors about half the rate of discount brokers, and a quarter the rate of full service brokers on most trades. These firms are principally bare-bones order takers. They are often used by market experts, who know what they want and do not need advice. Examples of deep-discount brokers include National Discount Brokers, Brown & Co., and Waterhouse Securities.

The emergence of the Internet has created a new category, on-line brokers, with commissions as low as 5 percent of the traditional brokerage commissions (see Key 27). There are now 140 on-line brokerages, many of which trade options. Examples include E*Trade, Ameritrade, and Mr. Stock.

Opening an account with a brokerage firm is similar in some respects to opening a bank account. A prospective investor must provide name, address, occupation, social security number, citizenship, proof of age, and a bank or financial reference. However, if the account is to trade on listed options, information on income, net worth, and investment experience is required. In addition, the prospective investor must acknowledge receipt of a current Options Clearing Corporation (OCC) prospectus and sign an "options agreement" verifying the data on the account form.

An investor who decides to trade options must first contact a broker and request a quote. The quote consists of two numbers: (1) the bid price (the highest price anyone is willing to pay) and (2) the ask price (the lowest price at which anyone is willing to sell). The investor can choose from among several types of orders:

1. *Market order.* The investor receives the best price available when the order is executed. Market orders are used by investors who want to establish option positions or get out of existing option positions. Investors who enter market orders are often disappointed at the executed price. To avoid these

situations, all the exchanges permit investors to place limit orders.

2. *Limit order.* A limit order stipulates that an options trade can be executed only at a specific price.

3. *Stop order.* A stop order is a very effective tool for preventing an investor from becoming too emotionally attached to a position. A stop order to sell becomes a market order when an option sells at or below the stop price (premium). A stop order to buy becomes a market order when an option sells at or above the stop price. For example, suppose ten XYZ January 34 call options are bought at a premium of $5. To protect at least part of the investment, the broker can be instructed to enter a sell stop order for the options at $3. Should the options drop to $3, the sell stop order is converted into a market order to sell at the best price currently available.

All orders are *day orders* unless otherwise indicated. A day order is good for the day of entry only. An investor also can choose to place a "good until canceled order," which means that the order remains in effect until executed or canceled.

Some brokers claim to be experts in options when in fact they are not. A broker who has not specialized in trading options for at least three years is not experienced in trading options. Brokers are anxious to handle options trades for two reasons:

1. The commissions on options are higher than commissions on common stock trades.

2. Options trading involves much more activity than trading in common stocks. Most listed options expire within nine months, and many of the more popular options expire even more quickly. In addition, options traders turn their money over much faster than stock traders. Investors who buy common stocks or bonds may hold them for years.

Therefore, a broker's word alone about options expertise is insufficient. Start by finding out who the firm's specialists are. Then arrange for an interview with one of them. This interview should not be conducted during trading hours when the broker may be busy and distracted. Prepare a list of questions concerning both the options market and the broker's experience in options trading.

Another tip in dealing with full-service brokerage firms involves commissions. Do not necessarily accept the list price. Since 1975, commissions have been negotiable. Most major brokerage firms now permit their brokers to grant discounts. In many cases, discounts are pegged to the client's volume of business.

26

INFORMATION ON OPTIONS

Options are not for casual investors. To profit from trading options requires study, strategy, and discipline about implementing the strategy. Options positions should be carefully selected and constantly monitored. Before allocating capital to options, investors should test their ideas on paper.

Fortunately, a large amount of information is available to assist investors in becoming successful options traders. Good starting points are the exchanges that trade options. All the exchanges provide packets of information at no charge. Investors can contact the exchanges either by phone or Web site:

- American Stock Exchange
  800-THE-AMEX
  www.amex.com
- Chicago Board Options Exchange
  800-OPTIONS
  www.cboe.com
- Pacific Exchange
  800-TALK-PSE
  www.pacifex.com
- Philadelphia Stock Exchange
  800-THE-PHLX
  www.phlx.com

The Internet has some excellent advisory services, several of which are discussed in Key 27. In addition, several publications are worthy of note. *Barron's* is a weekly financial publication that provides an exhaustive source of statistical data on all securities as well as options and futures. An excellent column "The Strike Price" is included in each issue. Although the column makes no specific recommendations, it reports the recommendations of other brokers and trackers. *Barron's* costs $145 per year and can be purchased by calling 800-822-7229.

Futures is a monthly magazine devoted to futures, options, and derivatives traders (888-898-5514). The $39 yearly subscription includes three special issues: (1) a directory of futures and options industry businesses in January, (2) *The Guide to Computerized Trading* in June, and (3) a trading issue in September. *Futures* also has an excellent Web site (www.futuresmag.com), which includes the latest issue of the magazine with full text of selected stories available, daily updates with commentary on hot markets, a chat room, spreadsheet downloads, a library of articles, market news, and links to other sites.

Those interested in technical analysis should find the monthly magazine *Technical Analysis of Stocks and Commodities* to be worthwhile reading. One section called "Websites for Traders" is particularly useful. A subscription costing $64.95 per year can be obtained by calling 800-832-4642.

For novices in options trading, two excellent books are available. Scott Pullman's *Options: A Personal Seminar* (Prentice-Hall, 1992) presents lucid discussions of the basic strategies, which are illustrated with examples, worksheets, and suggested guidelines for implementing these techniques. Michael Thomsett's *Getting Started in Options* (John Wiley & Sons, 1997) is an updated guide to trading and investing in options for the beginner. In clear, nontechnical language, it explains the basic terminology of options trading, and includes explanations of the most useful strategies for investors.

For a more advanced discussion of option trading, consider Lawrence McMillan's *McMillan on Options*

(John Wiley & Sons, 1996). This book provides a thorough coverage of pricing strategies, hedging techniques, options philosophy, volatility, and risk control. This book should be read only *after* the fundamentals of trading options are understood.

27

OPTIONS ON LINE

The 19 percent average annual increase in the S&P 500 Stock Index in the nineties has encouraged many investors to explore the world of options trading. This interest is further heightened by multimillion-dollar marketing and advertising campaigns, sponsored by options exchanges, to promote the potentially risky securities as mainstream investments. At Charles Schwab, options trading accounts for about 10 percent of retail revenue, up from 5 percent just two years ago.

The on-line brokerage industry has played an important role by not only making options trading much cheaper, but also making it easier than ever to research, trade, and track options. At leading Internet broker E*Trade, options trading volume has more than quadrupled in the past two years and accounts for 25 percent of its commission revenue.

Increasingly, traders are demanding more sophisticated options services. On-line brokers now permit stop orders on options, which require the option to be sold automatically if it reaches a preset price. E*Trade, Mr. Stock, and Web Street Securities are setting up Internet software that will allow complex options trades. For example, they want to make it easier to enter orders for complex spreads and straddles (see Keys 20 and 21), which call for the simultaneous purchase or sale of various options.

Commissions. Commissions on options used to be steep, eating up 7 to 10 percent of the amount invested. But the last five years have seen a huge decline in the cost of trading options. Commissions charged by major on-line brokers are as follows:

Broker	Commissions
E*Trade www.etrade.com	$20 per trade plus $1.75 per contact for any contract price, with a $29 minimum per options order.
Schwab www.schwab.com	$39 per trade with a percentage of the principal added on, depending on the total amount of the trade.
Mr. Stock www.mrstock.com	$19.95 per trade, plus $1.75 for each contract.
Web Street Securities www.WebStreetSecurities.com	$14.95 per trade, plus $1.75 per contract.
Fidelity Investments www.fidelity.com	$34.25, plus $1.75 per contract.

Full-service brokers charge two to five times the commissions charged by the Internet and traditional discount brokers.

The downward trend in fees is expected to continue. The options exchanges are edging away from the traditional system of traders screaming at one another on the floor toward electronic trading, enabling them to slash what they charge customers. Further, new competitors specializing in electronic trading are on the horizon, which also is expected to put downward pressure on pricing.

Exchange Information. The first place to look for information on line about options is at the excellent Web sites maintained by the exchanges:

- Chicago Board Options Exchange
  (www.cboe.com)
- American Stock Exchange (www.amex.com)
- Pacific Exchange (www.pacificex.com)
- Philadelphia Stock Exchange (www.phlx.com)

The CBOE, the world's largest options marketplace, is a particularly good starting point. The Web site has a price area in which the stock's symbol is entered, producing a view of the entire options chain (a list of all tradable options on a given stock), the last prices, bid, ask, net change, volume, and open interest.

Open interest is the number of open contracts of a particular option at any given time. Open interest in an option series has basically the same meaning as float does in a stock. Float refers to the number of shares outstanding and available for trading by the public. The number of open contracts is a measure of market interest. In options with lower open interest, the spread between the bid and ask prices usually is going to be greater, and there will be fewer investors available to take the other side of the trade.

The CBOE has organized all the elements of the Web site that options investors would find useful and put them in the "Trader's Tools." In that area, charts, news, company information, and historical volatility data (see Key 23) are available. The site contains an education area that provides a complete overview of options trading. Investors who desire more detailed information can click on "Bookstore" for a recommended list of books. In addition, there is a section on strategies, which describes some of the most common techniques employed by traders.

Other Information. The Options Industry Council (www.optionscentral.com) was created by the exchanges to promote options trading. This extremely useful site provides a tremendous array of free information, including videotapes and software. Free seminars and workshops are presented all over the United States, which are listed. Clicking on "Strategy of the Month" provides an informative essay on some aspect of options trading.

OptionSource (www.optionsource.com) is run by Bernie Schaeffer, a prominent authority on options trading. The site contains extensive tutorial materials that discuss options. Free daily market analysis and free quotes are provided. A daily analysis service, *Schaeffer on Options*, costs $255 per month or $2,995 for a one-year subscription. His most popular newsletter, the monthly *Option Advisor*, costs $119 per year. Beginners can start by taking lessons in what is called "Options 101." In addition, a trader employed by the newsletter offers a daily "Play of the Day." Subscribers can chat with one another on the message board. The monthly subscription fee is $39.95 per month. A free two-week trial is available for interested investors.

28

SPECIFICATIONS

The purpose of this Key is to provide specifications for certain actively traded options.

Specifications for All Equity Options

Unit of Trade: 100 shares per option contract.

Premium Quotations: Stated in points and fractions. One point equals $100. Minimum tick for series trading below $3 is ¹⁄₁₆ ($6.25), and for all other series, ⅛ ($12.50).

Strike Price Intervals: 2½ points for stocks trading between $5 and $25, 5 points for those trading from $25 to $200, and 10 points for those trading above $200.

Exercise Style: American-style—option may be exercised on any business day prior to the expiration date.

Expiration Months: Two near-term months plus two additional months of the January, February, or March quarterly cycle.

Expiration Dates: The Saturday immediately following the third Friday of the expiration month.

Position Limits: Maximum number of options that may be held by a single customer. Limits vary according to the number of outstanding shares and trading volume. The largest, most frequently traded stocks have an options position limit of 25,000 contracts; smaller capitalization stocks may offer position limits of 20,000, 10,500, 7,500, or 4,500 contracts.

Minimum Customer Margin for Uncovered Writers: The dollar amount of the premium plus 20 percent of the underlying security value minus the amount by which the option is out of the money (if any).

Trading Hours: 9:30 A.M. to 4:02 P.M. (Eastern Time).

Exercise Settlement Price: Strike price times $100.

Exercise Settlement Time: Exercise notices tendered on any business day will result in delivery of the underlying stock on the third business day following exercise.

Specifications for Equity LEAPS

Exchanges: AMEX, CBOE, PHLX, PCX.

Description: Equity LEAPS are American-style options on certain equities that have terms of up to three years. With the exception of the specifications listed below, equity LEAPS specifications are the same as those for regular-term equity options. Equity LEAPS have unique symbols to distinguish them from their corresponding regular-term options. Visit the exchange Web sites (see Key 26) for the most recent LEAPS symbols.

Strike Price Intervals: 2½ points when the strike price is between $5 and $25, 5 points when the strike price is over $25, 10 points when the strike price is over $200. Strikes are adjusted for splits, recapitalizations, and so on.

Expiration Dates: All equity LEAPS expire in January.

Position and Exercise Limits: Positions must be aggregated with those of any other option on the same underlying security for the purpose of position and exercise limits.

Premium Quotation: Stated in points and fractions. One point equals $100. Minimum tick for series trading below $3 is ⅟₁₆ ($6.25) and for all other series, ⅛ ($12.50).

Margin: Uncovered options writers must deposit 100 percent of the option proceeds plus 20 percent of the aggregate contract value (current equity price times $100) minus the amount by which the option is out of the money, if any. Long puts or calls must be paid in full.

29

FUTURES

The most risky and speculative of all the markets in the investment arena is the futures market. A futures contract is an agreement between two parties that commits one party to sell a commodity or security to the other at a given price and on a specified future date. Futures contracts are based upon an ever-expanding list of commodities that include agricultural products, metals, petroleum, financial instruments, foreign currencies, and stock indexes. In addition, the futures market now includes options on futures contracts, which enable options buyers to participate in futures markets with predetermined risks.

Futures make it possible to transfer risk from those who want to avoid it (hedgers) to those who are willing to accept it (speculators). Hedgers are individuals or firms that make purchases and sales in the futures market solely for the purpose of establishing a price level—weeks or months in advance—for something they later intend to buy or sell in the cash market (see Key 31). Their purpose is to protect themselves against the risk of an unfavorable price change in the interim.

The first organized commodity exchange in the United States was the Chicago Board of Trade (CBOT), founded in Chicago in 1848. The CBOT was originally intended as a central market for the conduct of cash grain business, and it was not until 1865 that the first futures transaction was performed there. Today, the CBOT has over 41 percent of all contracts traded in the United States.

Financial futures were not introduced until the 1970s. In 1976, the International Monetary Market (IMM), a subsidiary of the Chicago Mercantile Exchange (CME), began the 90-day Treasury bill futures contract (see Key

33). The following year, the CBOT initiated the Treasury bond futures contract. In 1981, the IMM created the Eurodollar futures contract.

A major financial futures milestone was reached in 1982, when the Kansas City Board of Trade introduced a stock index futures contract based upon the Value Line Stock Index. This offering was followed in short order by the introduction of the S&P 500 Index futures contract on the Chicago Mercantile Exchange and the New York Stock Exchange Composite Index traded on the New York Futures Exchange. In October 1997, futures based upon the Dow Jones Industrial Average were introduced. All of these contracts provide for cash delivery rather than delivery of securities.

Trading volume on the futures exchange has surged in the last three decades—from 3.9 million contracts in 1960 to 503.2 million contracts in 1998. In their short history, financial futures have become the dominant factor in the futures markets. In 1998, 70 percent of all futures contracts traded were financial futures. The two most actively traded futures contracts are (1) the Treasury bond contract traded on the CBOT and (2) the Eurodollar contract traded on the CME.

Trading in futures is regulated by the Commodity Futures Trading Commission (CFTC), an independent federal agency consisting of five commissioners appointed by the President. The CFTC serves as an overseer by determining that self-regulation is continuous and effective.

The National Futures Association (NFA), formed in 1982, is a congressionally authorized self-regulatory organization subject to CFTC oversight. It polices activities of both exchange member firms and nonmember firms throughout the futures industry. In addition, the NFA has the responsibility for registering persons and firms that are required to be registered with the CFTC.

It is illegal for any person or firm to offer futures contracts for purchase or sale unless those contracts are traded on one of the nation's regulated futures exchanges and the person or firm is registered with the CFTC. In addition, persons and firms conducting futures-related business with the public must be NFA members. Therefore, an investor should be extremely cautious if approached by a party attempting to sell a futures-related investment unless it can be verified that the party is registered with the CFTC and is an NFA member. Verification is accomplished by phoning the NFA toll-free at 800-621-3570.

Futures often are confused with options, but important differences exist between the two types of instruments. An option permits the buyer to choose whether or not to exercise the option by a specified date. In other words, with an option, the buyer purchases a right, and only the writer takes on an obligation. On the other hand, with futures, both sides take on an obligation. A futures contract obligates the buyer to buy and the seller to sell at the agreed-upon price on the agreed-upon date.

In addition, the buyer of an option pays a premium to acquire the option. In a futures transaction, neither party pays a premium. Both parties must put up a good-faith deposit to guarantee fulfillment of the purchase or sale obligation. This good-faith deposit is called *margin*.

Futures trading is the riskiest sector of the investment arena. Even successful traders lose money on more than half of their trades. The key to their success lies in cutting their losses short on losing trades and staying with the profitable trades long enough to more than offset all the small losses. This feature of futures is one reason speculators with less than $50,000 in their accounts are seldom successful. The accounts are not large enough to withstand a series of small losses. Research shows that the size of a trading account is related to success in futures trading. Investors with small amounts of capital should avoid this market altogether. Those investors with considerable resources should limit their exposure to no more than 5 to 10 percent of their capital.

Only 1 to 2 percent of all futures contacts actually result in delivery. Very few speculators have the desire to take delivery of 5,000 bushels of corn, 60,000 pounds of soybean oil, or even $100,000 of Treasury notes. As a result, gains and losses generally are realized by buying or selling offsetting futures contracts prior to the delivery date. If delivery does occur, it takes the form of a negotiable instrument (such as a warehouse receipt) that proves the holder's ownership of the commodity.

The sale of a contract that was previously purchased liquidates a futures contract in the same way that the sale of 100 shares of GM stock liquidates an earlier purchase of 100 shares of GM stock. In a similar vein, a futures contract that was initially sold can be liquidated by an offsetting purchase. In any event, a gain or loss is computed by taking the difference between the buying price and the selling price.

Cash-settlement futures contracts are contracts that are settled in cash rather than by delivery at the time the contract expires. For example, stock index futures are settled in cash based upon the index number at the close of the final day of trading. No provision exists for delivery of the shares of stock that make up the index.

After the closing bell signals the end of a day's trading, the exchange's clearing organization matches each purchase made that day with the corresponding sale and computes each member's gains or losses based upon that day's price changes. The system of daily settlement in the futures markets is called "mark to market" and is conducted through an intermediary body called the futures clearinghouse. Each firm then computes the gains and losses for each of its customers with futures contracts.

Gains and losses on futures contracts are credited and deducted on a daily basis. For example, a $1,000 profit resulting from the day's price changes is immediately credited to the trader's account and could be withdrawn. Alternatively, a $500 loss resulting from the day's price changes would be immediately debited to the customer's account for that amount. This daily cash settlement is a significant feature of futures trading.

Long vs. Short. The buyer of a futures contract is said to be long, or has a long position (unless the purchase is to offset and thus close out an existing short position). The seller of a futures contract is said to be short, or has a short position (unless the sale is closing out a long position). A speculator sells a futures contract short because of a belief that the market is headed lower and the futures contract can be purchased back later at a lower price.

In futures, there is a short position for every long position. If an investor buys a futures contract, another market participant is selling the same contract. If an investor sells a futures contract short, another investor must buy it. Gains on one side of a futures contract must be counterbalanced by losses on the other side of the position. Like options, futures are a zero-sum game. When the longs win, the shorts lose, and vice versa.

30

LEVERAGE

Investors should recognize the extreme risk associated with investing in futures. No other form of investment or speculation is so highly leveraged. An understanding of how leverage magnifies the risks and opportunities associated with the trading of futures is crucial to an understanding of these investment vehicles.

The leverage of futures trading results from the fact that only a relatively small amount of money (known as initial margin) is required to buy or sell a futures contract. For example, a deposit of only $2,000 might enable an investor to buy a futures contract representing $35,000 worth of cotton. The initial margin is typically 5 to 15 percent of the value of the underlying contract, although in some cases it is even less. The smaller the margin in relationship to the value of the futures contract, the greater the leverage and the greater the risk.

High leverage can produce large profits when compared to the initial margin if the speculator correctly anticipates the future price change. Alternatively, if prices move in the opposite direction from what was anticipated, large losses can result. Leverage is a double-edged sword.

EXAMPLE:
Suppose that an investor anticipates rising stock prices and buys one October S&P 500 Stock Index futures contract at a time when the S&P is trading at 1,400. The initial margin required is $23,000. Because the value of the S&P futures contract is calculated by multiplying the current level of the S&P 500 by $250, the contract includes $350,000 ($250 × 1,400) of secu-

rities, and each point change in the index represents a $250 gain or loss.

Therefore, an increase in the index from 1,400 to 1,492 (6.5 percent) would double the investment (92 points × $250 a point), and a decrease from 1,400 to 1,308 would wipe out the investment. The 100 percent gain or loss resulted from only a 6.5 percent change in the index. Keep in mind that a 6.5 percent change is equivalent to a 715-point change in the Dow Jones Industrial Average if it stands at 11,000, and a 91-point drop in the S&P 500 if it stands at 1,400. A 6.5 percent change in the index is well within the range of probability.

Although a futures contract provides exactly the same actual profit (dollar amount) as owning or selling short the actual commodities or securities represented by the contract, the low initial margin magnifies the percentage profit or loss potential. In this market, speculators must be prepared for the possibility of losing their investment in a single day. An investor who is not reconciled to that possibility should avoid this market altogether.

31

HEDGING IN FUTURES

Hedging is the fundamental purpose of the futures markets. Many of the rules that govern futures contracts are designed to reflect the hedging needs of commercial interests. Although the details of hedging transactions can be complex, the principle is simple. Hedging involves individuals and firms that make purchases and sales in the futures market to reduce the risk of loss from price fluctuations of the asset in the cash market. The purpose is to protect themselves against the risk of an unfavorable price change in the interim.

The position taken in the futures market is generally opposite and approximately equal to the one held in the cash market. A long position in the futures market—called a "long hedge"—protects against a possible price increase in the commodity (including securities). A long hedge would be used by an individual or a firm that is short the actual commodity. For example, an exporter who has promised delivery in several months at an agreed-upon price could engage in a long hedge.

A short position in the futures market—called a "short hedge"—is designed to protect against a possible decrease in the price of the commodity. A short hedge would be executed by a firm or individual who is long in the actual commodity. For example, a hog breeder who will bring animals to market in several months is said to be long in the cash market. The breeder could go short (sell futures contracts) in the CME live-hog futures market to protect against the possibility of a decrease in the price of live hogs when they are ready for market.

Hedging techniques are popular with institutional and other professional investors. Stock index futures can be used to hedge a stock portfolio so that the potential for both profits and/or losses is eliminated. If there is concern about a future market decline, hedging may be preferred to actually selling stocks. The reasons include the following:

1. The tax consequences might be significant.
2. Substantial dividends could be lost.
3. Commission costs may be too high.
4. There is uncertainty about the prospect of decline.
5. The decline is expected to be temporary.

The S&P 500 futures contract can be used to hedge a portfolio of stocks. To provide a rough-coverage hedge for a portfolio, divide the portfolio value by the current index value times $250. This result is the number of contracts that is equal in value to the stock portfolio. However, this position might not completely hedge a portfolio because a stock portfolio can change in value to a different degree than the stock index.

EXAMPLE:
Suppose that the manager of a $70 million portfolio is concerned about the short-term market outlook and is willing to give up the potential for gains to protect against possible losses. If the index stands at 1,400, one would need to sell 200 contracts [$70 million ÷ (1,400 × $250)]. If the market declines, the gain on the contracts offsets the decline in the portfolio value. If the market rises, the decline in the futures prices offsets the gain on the stock portfolio owned. The hedge can be eliminated at any time by buying back 200 contracts to cancel out those sold.

32

COMMODITY FUTURES

A commodity futures contract is an agreement covering the purchase and sale of physical goods for future delivery on a commodity exchange. The futures contract requires the future seller to deliver to a designated location a specified quantity of a commodity to be sold to the future buyer at a stipulated price on some specified later date. Originally, the purpose of futures was to transfer risk from one party to another and to protect against price fluctuations. Subsequently, speculation has become an important factor in these markets.

Commodity futures are used primarily by four groups of people: (1) producers, (2) consumers, (3) investors, and (4) exchange-floor traders. Producers use the futures market to protect the price they receive for their products. These people range from small farmers to managers of giant companies. To illustrate, a farmer who thinks the price of corn may decline by harvest time can sell corn futures early in the season. If the price of corn declines, a profit on the futures contract will compensate for the lower price received for the harvest. This transaction is an example of hedging.

Consumers can use futures to protect themselves against a rise in the price of commodities. These consumers range from food processors to individuals who buy corn or automobiles. To illustrate, a popcorn manufacturer who thinks the price of corn is going to rise, thus intensifying competition with potato chips or alternative snacks, may buy corn futures for delivery a year later. If the price of corn rises, the profit on the futures compensates for the higher price paid for the corn. If the price falls, the futures losses are offset by the lower cost of corn. In either case, the popcorn manufacturer has a hedged position that offers protection from fluctuations in the price of corn.

Investors use futures to speculate on future price changes. Theoretically, the speculator assumes the price risk that the hedger is seeking to minimize. When the hedger sells futures, it is the speculator who buys; when the hedger buys futures, it is the speculator who sells. Speculators generally attempt to make short-term profits on a large number of transactions. Typically, the hedger makes a smaller number of transactions and holds each position for a longer period of time. By making it easier for others to buy and sell futures, speculators help to make the market more liquid.

Recently, smaller investors have become more interested in commodity futures. They are lured by the tremendous leverage that investments in commodities provide. After certain net worth standards are met, only a small deposit, or margin, is required to buy or sell futures. The cash requirement varies from 3 to 15 percent of the contract. For example, $2,000 can buy $35,000 worth of a commodity.

As highly leveraged investments, futures present an opportunity for dramatic profits. However, it is a two-way street because an investor also may incur dramatic losses. A recent study of commodity speculators revealed that 75 percent lose money. Therefore, the risks may outweigh the benefits for many investors.

Exchange-floor traders are another group of commodity futures users. They serve as middlemen by buying from producers and selling to users. As individuals trading for their own or a firm's account, these floor traders are an important factor in creating market activity in addition to ensuring that bids and offers are available.

The commodity futures market is very close to being a purely competitive market. There are many buyers and sellers, and none is large enough to determine prices. Prices are determined by supply and demand, which are influenced by a variety of forces. These forces involve a range of political, social, and economic factors, in addition to traits peculiar to the particular commodity. Gold is an example of a commodity with a price strongly influenced by political factors. Prices of most agricultural commodities are determined largely by fluctuations in supply.

Commodity futures markets function primarily as a form of forward pricing (guarantee of a price when delivery of the commodity occurs). Only about 2 percent of all futures contracts actually result in delivery. Typically, futures contracts change hands many times. However, one characteristic supporting the integrity of futures markets is that an investor may actually acquire or deliver a commodity.

33

FINANCIAL FUTURES

Although commodity futures have been traded on exchanges for more than a century, financial futures were not introduced until the 1970s. Financial futures are futures contracts written on securities, money, or stock indexes. Three main types of financial futures are traded: (1) interest rate futures, (2) stock index futures, and (3) currency futures. Unlike commodity futures, financial futures do not involve delivery of a physical property, but rather of financial securities or cash. Like commodity futures, financial futures are used by borrowers, lenders, and other users of financial instruments to hedge investments.

Investors can use positions in the financial futures market to protect the gains they have made in the cash market. Speculators can use financial futures to profit from anticipated changes in interest rates, foreign exchange rates, and movements in the stock market. However, caution is advised to inexperienced investors. All futures markets are dominated by professionals, many of whom employ sophisticated methods to determine their positions. Small investors in these markets do not have a high success rate.

Financial futures are traded on an exchange that has regulations to ensure the performance of contracts. The exchange clearinghouse acts as a third party to and guarantor of all transactions, thus eliminating the need for sellers and buyers to become known to one another. Although a future is a commitment to buy or sell at some point in the future, delivery of the underlying instrument rarely occurs. Trades in futures contracts are settled by entering into an offsetting position (a contract sold is closed out by a purchase and a contract bought is closed out by selling the contract).

Although the financial futures market is fairly young, about 65 percent of all futures traded in the United States in 1998 were financial futures. Interest-rate futures (e.g., Treasury bills, bonds, and notes) accounted for about 47 percent of all futures trades (see Key 38). In their relatively short existence, financial futures clearly have become the most exciting segment of the futures market.

Limitless hedging opportunities are available in the financial futures market. For example, borrowers can hedge against higher interest rates, and lenders against lower interest rates. Investors can hedge against an overall decline or rise in stock prices. Whatever the strategy, a hedger willingly surrenders the opportunity to benefit from favorable price changes in exchange for protection against unfavorable price changes.

Speculators are individuals or firms seeking to profit from anticipated increases or decreases in futures prices. Through trading in pursuit of profit, speculators help create a liquid market. An investor "goes long" by purchasing futures contracts in hopes of later selling them at a higher price. Alternatively, an investor "goes short" by selling futures contracts in hopes of later buying back identical and offsetting contracts at a lower price. With futures trading, the investor can profit from declining prices (by selling) or profit from rising prices (by buying).

34

OPTIONS ON FUTURES

Options on futures were introduced to the investing community in 1982. Recognizing the success of the CBOE and the stock exchanges in trading options, the futures exchanges wanted a piece of the action. Options on futures are the financial instruments that permit futures exchanges to also trade options. In 1998, over 127 million such contracts were traded, with interest rate options comprising about ⅔ of that total.

An option on a future gives the buyer the right, but not the obligation, to buy or sell a particular futures contract at a stated price at any time prior to a specified date. As with ordinary options, there are two distinct types: (1) call options and (2) put options.

The buyer of a call option buys the right, but not the obligation, to purchase a particular futures contract at a stated price at any time during the life of the option. The buyer of a put option acquires the right, but not the obligation, to sell a particular futures contract at a stated price at any time during the life of the option. If the option is exercised, settlement is not in cash but through actual delivery of a futures contract.

Options on futures involve two sets of relationships: (1) the one between the futures contract and the underlying commodity, security, or index; and (2) the one between the option and the futures contract. The additional complication can make these instruments even more volatile than regular options. The average futures investor should not be assuming this additional risk. Only investors familiar with regular options should trade these instruments.

Another type of option on futures involves Treasury

bonds. This type of futures contract is based upon $100,000 face U.S. Treasury bonds. Prices of Treasury bonds and futures are quoted in terms of points and 32nds. Each full point is worth $1,000, and each 32nd is worth $31.25. Thus, a bond with a market value of $99,000 is quoted at 99–00. A bond quoted at 99–8 (99 and $\frac{8}{32}$) is worth $99,250. A bond futures contract quoted at 92–04 (92 and $\frac{4}{32}$) is worth $92,125.

Options on Treasury bond futures contracts are quoted differently from bond and bond futures prices. They are quoted in 64ths of a point. Each 64th is equal to $15.625. Thus, a premium quoted at 3–8 is 3 points and $\frac{8}{64}$, or $3,125. A premium of 4–32 (4 and $\frac{32}{64}$) is worth $4,500.

The principal attraction of options on futures as opposed to futures is that they offer an options buyer the potential for substantial profit while limiting the buyer's risk to the up-front cost (the premium) of the option. Any options strategy also can be applied to futures options. For example, if interest rates are expected to decline, calls can be purchased or the investor can write (sell) puts to earn the premium (see Keys 3 and 13). If interest rates are forecasted to rise, puts can be bought or calls can be written to earn the premium. In a stable interest-rate environment, covered calls (Key 10) can be written to earn additional income if cash bonds are held.

35

S&P 500 FUTURES

Stock index futures have enjoyed tremendous growth in trading volume since they were introduced in 1982. A stock index futures contract is a contract to buy or sell the face value of a stock index. The two principal stock index futures contracts traded in the United States are (1) Standard & Poor's (S&P) 500 Stock Index contract at the Chicago Mercantile Exchange (CME); and (2) S&P Mini Index contract at the CME (see Key 36). S&P 500 contracts, which are written on the S&P 500 Index, account for about 90 percent of all stock index futures trading.

The S&P 500 Index is designed to be an accurate proxy for a diversified portfolio of highly capitalized, blue-chip stocks. The index is based upon the stock prices of 500 different companies, including about 400 industrial, 40 utilities, 20 transportation companies, and 40 financial institutions. The market value of the 500 companies is approximately equal to 80 percent of the value of all stocks traded on the New York Stock Exchange (NYSE).

Although the Dow Jones Industrial Average (DJIA) receives greater attention from the media, the S&P 500 Index is recognized by most professional investors as the benchmark index. Because of the large number of companies it represents, its movement is more representative of the stock market as a whole than the DJIA, which consists of only 30 blue-chip companies. The S&P 500 Index consists primarily of NYSE-listed companies, but also includes some American Stock Exchange (AMEX) and NASDAQ stocks.

With S&P 500 futures, the commodity is a portfolio of stocks represented by a stock price index. Unlike physical commodities, which actually may be delivered, index futures involve a cash settlement of the difference between the original transaction price and the final price of the index at the termination of the contract.

The value of an S&P futures contract is calculated by multiplying the futures price by $250. For example, with a price of $1,400, the value of the contract would be $350,000 ($250 × $1,400). The minimum trading price change (called a *tick*) for the contract is $0.10. Therefore, if the S&P futures contract goes up a tick from $1,400 to $1,400.10, the value of the contract increases by $25 ($250 × .10).

The value of the futures price closely follows the value of the index, and the futures price will change as the underlying index changes. However, the price of the futures may be higher or lower than the index, depending upon market expectations as to future prices. A summary of S&P 500 futures contract terms are given below:

Contract:	S&P 500 Index
Size:	$250 × the S&P 500 Index
Minimum price change:	10 index points = $25 per contract
Delivery months:	March, June, September, December
Last day of trading:	Thursday prior to the third Friday of the contract month
Settlement procedure:	Cash

As previously mentioned, the futures market is a very fast game. Discipline is an absolute necessity for success. Investors must let their profits run and limit losses. The leveraged nature of this market makes for stunning changes in returns on margin.

EXAMPLE:
In a Rising Market. Investor Zeus is convinced that the market will rise in the next three months. The S&P

500 Index is at 1,400, and she buys a futures contract at $1,415 for delivery in three months. The S&P 500 Index contract represents a value of $250 times the price of the contract, for a total of $353,750 ($250 × 1,415). Assume that Zeus must put up a margin of $23,000. To trade in the futures markets, an investor is required to post a performance bond margin to ensure performance against the obligations of the futures contract. Minimum margin requirements represent a very small percentage of a contract's total value. In this case, the $23,000 margin only represents about 6.5 percent of the total contract value. Each point up or down brings her a return of $250. Two months later, the index has risen to 1,440 and her contract is selling for $1,450. If she decides to sell, her profit would equal 35 points, or $8,750. An $8,750 return on $23,000 margin is equal to 38 percent in only two months.

EXAMPLE:
In a Falling Market. Instead of rising, the contract price dropped to 1,385 after one month. At this point, Zeus has lost $7,500 (30 points × $250 per point) of the margin put up. She is likely to receive a margin call. Suppose she puts up additional margin and the contract price continues to drop to 1,360. The 55-point drop has eliminated $13,750 of her initial margin of $23,000. The total drop of only 3.9 percent (55 points/1,415) cost her 59.8 percent of her initial margin. Unfortunately, a 3.9 percent drop in the market is very possible, which is why investors in futures should be prepared for large losses.

36

E-MINI S&P 500 FUTURES

In September 1997, the Chicago Mercantile Exchange (CME) introduced a smaller version of the S&P 500 futures and options contracts, called the E-Mini (electronic mini) S&P 500. These new contracts are based upon the S&P 500 as are the S&P 500 futures but are a fraction of the size. The so-called "Mini" enables the individual investor to participate and profit from the benchmark index tracked by pension and mutual funds across the country. Typically, the margin required for this contract is about 20 percent of the margin required for the S&P 500 futures contract. The Mini has become extremely popular with individual investors and now ranks second to the S&P futures contract as the most actively traded stock index futures contract.

Mini S&P 500 futures are agreements to buy or sell the cash value of the S&P 500 Index at a specific future date. The contracts are valued at $50 times the futures price. For example, if the Mini S&P 500 futures price is at 1300.00, the value of the contract is $65,000 ($50 × 1300.00). In contrast, the S&P 500 futures contract is valued at $250 times the futures price.

The minimum price movement (called *tick*) of a contract is .25 index points, or $12.50 ($50 × .25) per contract. If the futures contract moves one tick, from 1300.00 to 1300.25, a long (buying) position would be credited for $12.50; a short (selling) position would be debited for $12.50.

Mini S&P 500 futures, like the standard S&P 500 futures, are cash settled; there is no delivery of the individual stocks. Further, Mini S&P 500 daily settlements and quarterly expirations will use the same exact price as the S&P 500 futures. The same daily settlement prices allow these contracts to benefit from the liquidity of the S&P 500 shares. Like the S&P 500, Mini S&P 500 positions are settled in cash on the third Friday of the quarterly contract month. The quarterly contract months are March, June, September, and December.

There also are options available on Mini S&P 500 futures. The dollar value of an option contract is $50 times the premium, or price, of the option. For example, if the December 1300.00 call has a premium of 8.00, the dollar value of the Mini S&P option would be $400 ($50 × 8.00). Strike prices for Mini S&P 500 options are in 5-point increments (e.g., 1310.00, 1315.00, 1320.00) for the two nearest contracts and 10-point intervals for the deferred months.

Like the CME's S&P 500 options contract, Mini S&P 500 options are settled on the third Friday of the contract month. Real-time (current) Mini S&P 500 quotes, such as the best bid, best offer, and the size of the best bid and best offer, may be viewed for free via the CME Web site (www.cme.com).

Mini S&P 500 futures and options are available for trading virtually 24 hours per day. The method of execution for these contracts is determined by the size of the order. Smaller Mini S&P orders will use electronic order entry, routing, and trade matching via GLOBEX, the CME's automated order entry and matching system. Larger orders will be executed by open outcry on the trading floor.

The CME issues several excellent publications that explain stock index futures and options on futures. To obtain these publications, call the CME (312-930-2351):

- *The Basics of CME Futures and Options* (brochure)
- *How to Get Started Trading CME Index Products* (brochure)
- *E-Mini S&P 500 Futures and Options* (brochure)
- *21 Proven Strategies for E-Mini S&P 500 Options* (brochure)
- *U.S. Equity Index Futures and Options* (information guide)

37

FUTURES ON THE DJIA

After refusing for many years, Dow Jones & Company in 1997 licensed trading in futures and futures options contracts. Both of these contracts trade on the Chicago Board of Trade (CBOT). Although the S&P 500 is favored by institutions, the Dow Jones Industrial Average (DJIA) is the most widely followed and recognized stock index by individual traders. The 30 stocks that comprise the DJIA—all household names that trade heavily in the United States as well as in major foreign stock markets—have a total market value of about $3 trillion and represent about one fifth of the market value of all U.S. stocks.

Although the DJIA is widely followed, its movement has been difficult to replicate because "buying the Dow" required buying shares in each of the 30 stocks. Further, it is even more difficult to "sell (short) the Dow." The introduction of the DJIA futures, however, permits participation in the broader market simply by buying or selling the futures contracts.

The value of a CBOT DJIA futures contract is equal to $10 times the current index level. For example, if the index level is at 11,000, holding a futures contract is equivalent to investing $110,000 in a portfolio of DJIA stocks. When a DJIA futures contract is traded, the seller is agreeing to sell $10 times the index and the buyer is agreeing to buy $10 times the index on the expiration date of the contract. In other words, the minimum price fluctuation (called *tick size*) in a DJIA futures contract is one point, or $10.

The standardized contract months are based upon a quarterly trading cycle, with expirations in March, June,

September, and December. Settlement occurs on the third Friday of the contract month. If an open position is held, it can be liquidated, or offset, at any point prior to settlement simply by initiating the opposite trade (short or long) in the same contract month.

Futures Options. A futures contract creates an obligation to assume a position. Unlike futures, options on futures give the right, but not the obligation, to assume a futures position at a predetermined price. Buying a put option gives the right to short futures, whereas a call purchase gives the right to long futures. The price paid for the rights conferred by an option is called the *option premium*. For example, a call at a strike price of 11,000 allows an investor to become long one futures contract at a strike price of 11,000. A put at the same strike price entitles an investor to become short one futures contract at 11,000.

The seller (writer) of a call or put is obligated to enter a futures position if the buyer chooses to exercise the option. If an investor is short one call and the long exercises, that trader becomes short one futures contract at 11,000. If an investor is short one put and the long exercises, that investor is long one futures contract at 11,000.

The CBOT lists options on the DJIA futures at 100-point strike intervals following the same March, June, September, and December futures trading cycle. For example, a June call option with a strike price of 11,000 gives the right to enter a long futures position with a value of $110,000 at any time up to the option's expiration in June.

Project A. On May 2, 1998, the DJIA futures and options on futures were made available on Project A, the CBOT's after-hours electronic trading system. Project A is an electronic order entry and matching system that operates outside regular floor trading hours. This system permits the round-the-clock trading of futures. The principal CBOT financial contracts are actively traded on project A (e.g., futures and options on Treasury bonds;

10-, 5-, and 2-year Treasury notes; futures on 30-day fed funds; and futures and options on municipal bonds). The volume growth on Project A since its introduction in 1994 has indeed been impressive. The average daily volume has increased from less than 2,000 contracts in 1994 to 44,575 contracts in 1998. To access Project A, customers simply call their brokers and place orders using the same procedure as for orders placed during regular hours.

38

TREASURY BOND FUTURES

Futures contracts can be bought for all three Treasury securities: bonds, notes, and bills. Treasury bonds mature in 30 years; notes mature in periods from 2 to 10 years; and bills mature in periods up to 12 months. In addition, there also is a very active futures market in Eurodollars, which are U.S. dollars on deposit outside of the United States.

In 1998, the Treasury bond future on the Chicago Board of Trade (CBOT) was the most actively traded futures contract (112 million contracts), slightly ahead of the Eurodollar contract (109 million contracts) traded on the Chicago Mercantile Exchange (CME). The popularity of these bonds can be attributed to several factors. First, the massive deficits of the U.S. government have required the issuance of many Treasury bonds. In addition, Treasury bonds have become the benchmark for long-term interest rates to which other long-term rates are tied. Thus, prices of Treasury bond futures are a sensitive barometer of long-term interest rates. Treasury bond futures are widely used to hedge against the risk of bond holding.

Over 40,000 Treasury bond futures contracts were traded daily at the CBOT in 1998. A contract is for future delivery of a $100,000 face value Treasury bond. In actuality, futures traders rarely take delivery of Treasury bonds, and most trades are canceled by making an offsetting trade.

The Treasury bond futures contract accepts delivery of U.S. Treasury securities with maturities or earliest call dates at least 15 years in the future. Delivery is allowed at any time during the delivery month. The last day of trading is the eighth-to-the-last business day of the delivery month. A summary of U.S. Treasury bond contract terms follows:

Exchange:	Chicago Board of Trade
Quantity:	$100,000 face value
Delivery months:	March, June, September, December
Delivery specifications:	Delivery of U.S. Treasury bonds with maturity value of at least 15 years if not callable, and if callable, with a first call date no earlier than 15 years from the first day of the delivery month. Call date is the first date on which the bond can be retired at the election of the issuer.
Minimum price movement:	32nds of a point, or $31.25 per contract

Many institutions have large bond holdings that they use to hedge against interest-rate risk. A rise in interest rates pushes down the price of bonds, whereas declining interest rates raise bond prices. An investor who is concerned that interest rates are about to spurt upward can sell Treasury bond futures. If bond prices later decline, the price of bond futures also drops, enabling the investor to buy back the futures for less. If bond prices rise, the investor loses money on the futures but makes money on the bonds.

Inexperienced individual investors should avoid this market. Trading is dominated by institutions and dealers in Treasury securities who use sophisticated trading systems. Because professionals generally play this market, the margin required usually is less than that for stock index futures. Lower margin means higher leverage and greater risk.

39

MARGIN

The term "margin" as applied to common stocks has an altogether different meaning when applied to futures. Margin on common stocks refers to the use of borrowed funds to supplement the investor's own money. The investor makes only partial payment for his/her stocks and borrows the rest. Therefore, trading on margin essentially is trading on credit.

In the futures arena, margin is simply a deposit of good-faith money that can be drawn upon by the brokerage firm to cover losses that may be incurred in the course of futures trading. Both the buyer and seller of a futures contract are required to provide margin. The purpose of margin is to ensure contract performance and the integrity of the marketplace. It should be noted that stock options cannot be purchased on margin.

Minimum margin requirements for each futures contract are set by the exchange on which the contract is traded. Exchanges can adjust the margin requirements as market conditions and risks change. Also, individual brokerage firms may require margins that are higher than those required by the exchange. Generally, the margin required is about 5 to 10 percent of the current value of the futures contract.

Initial margin (sometimes called *original margin*) is the amount of money that a customer must deposit with a brokerage firm at the time a futures position is established. Depending on exchange requirements, initial margin may consist of cash, funds transferred from another of the customer's accounts, U.S. government securities, a letter of credit, or a negotiable warehouse receipt.

In addition to prescribing minimum margin levels, the exchange sets the *maintenance margin* requirement. The maintenance margin is the amount of money that must be maintained on deposit while a futures position is open. If profits accrue on an open position, they are added to the balance in the margin account. When losses are incurred, they are deducted from the balance in the margin account. If the funds in a margin account are reduced by losses to below the maintenance margin requirement, the broker will require that additional money be deposited to bring the account back up to the initial margin. Requests for additional margin are termed *margin calls*. The amount of maintenance margin varies by exchange, but the 75 percent level is a common standard.

EXAMPLE:

Suppose that the initial margin required to open a futures contract is $2,000 and that the maintenance margin requirement is $1,500. If losses on the open position reduce the balance in the account to $1,450, then the broker would issue a margin call for $550 to restore the account to the initial margin of $2,000.

Futures traders must understand the brokerage firm's margin agreement and know how and when the firm expects margin calls to be met. Delivering margin calls to futures participants is the responsibility of the broker. If a margin call is not met within a suitable period of time, the firm can protect itself by liquidating the investor's open positions at the available market price.

40

ORDERS

Orders to buy or sell futures contracts are either market orders or contingent orders. A *market order* is an order to buy or sell a futures contract at the best possible price as soon as possible. *Contingent orders* include instructions that make their execution dependent upon certain conditions, such as time or price limit. Each futures order should contain the following items of information:

1. Whether to buy or sell
2. The number of contracts to be bought or sold
3. The relevant futures contract, including both delivery month and year
4. Whether it is a market order or a contingent order

Although there are many different types of contingent orders, we will describe only the most important ones. The most common contingent order is a *limit order*. Limit orders are executed only at a price specified by the customer (or a better price). A limit order to buy may be filled only at or below the limit price, whereas a limit order to sell may be filled only at or above the limit price. Many investors place limit orders because they are dissatisfied with the prices they receive when they place market orders. However, a limit order provides no assurance of execution. If the limit price is not reached, the order will not be filled.

A *stop order* (sometimes referred to as a *stop loss order*) is an order that becomes a market order when a particular price level is reached. A sell stop is placed below the market and a buy stop is placed above the market. Stop loss orders are used to limit the amount lost if the futures price moves against a position. For example, if an investor buys an S&P 500 contract at $1,400 and wishes to limit possible losses, then a stop order might be placed to sell an offsetting contract if the price should drop to $1,350. If the contract price does drop to $1,350, a stop order becomes an order to execute the trade at the best price currently available.

However, there is no guarantee that it will be possible to execute the order at the price specified in the stop order. In a volatile market, the market price may be declining or rising so rapidly that there is no opportunity to liquidate a position at the stop price designated. The broker's only obligation, under these conditions, is to execute the order at the best price available.

In addition to limiting losses, stop orders also can be used to protect profits. For example, if an investor bought S&P 500 futures at $1,400 and the price is now $1,500, then a stop order might be issued to sell if and when the price drops to $1,475. This order, subject to the previously described limitations of stop orders, could protect most of the profit while still permitting gains from continued price increases.

41

READING FUTURES PRICES

Exhibit 3 is an example of how futures prices are reported. The second boldfaced line gives the name of the commodity—in this case, corn. Also listed is the exchange, CBT, which stands for the Chicago Board of Trade. Finally, the line lists the size of a single contract (5,000 bushels) and the way in which prices are quoted (cents per bushel).

The first column gives the months in which the delivery of the contract may occur. Trading usually is limited to certain specified months and to less than two years in the future. The next three columns give the opening, highest, and lowest prices of the day. A blank indicates that a particular month has not traded that day. The fifth column gives the settlement price, the price brokers use for valuing portfolios and for deciding whether to call for more margin.

The next column, titled "Change," shows the difference between the latest settlement price and the settlement price for the previous day. The second and third columns from the right display the highest and lowest prices at which each contract has been traded. The right-hand column shows the open interest. Open interest is the number of contracts outstanding; it is a measure of the public interest in a contract. The open interest is computed by exchanges after each trading day.

The decimal point must be included to interpret the prices. For example, a price of 215 means $2.15 per bushel. To calculate a change in the value of a contract caused by a price change, contract size must be considered. Because the contract size of corn is 5,000 bushels, each point change means $50 (5,000 × .01).

Among the most actively traded futures contracts are those covering Treasury bonds (see Key 38). Treasury bonds, which are Treasury securities maturing in more than ten years, are traded on the Chicago Board of Trade (see Exhibit 4). Underlying the futures contract is $100,000 worth of Treasury bonds. Bonds are quoted in 32nds of one percent of this face value. Thus, a price of 103–12 means 103 and 12⁄32 or 103⅜ ($103,375).

For these futures, the lifetime high and low columns are replaced by a column for yields based upon settlement prices and the change in this yield from the previous day. The yield is the interest rate based upon its current price, original interest rate, and remaining life. Because many speculators focus upon interest rates rather than bond prices, these columns frequently are of greater interest than the prices.

EXHIBIT 3
Futures Price Quotations

Open Interest Reflects Previous Trading Day.

GRAINS AND OILSEEDS

	Open	High	Low	Settle	Chg	Lifetime High	Lifetime Low	Open Interest
				CORN (CBT) 5,000 bu.; cents per bu.				
July	181	182½	177	180	+ 1	312	177	3,198
Sept	187½	189¾	184	186¾	+ ½	280	184	105,756
Dec	198¾	200	194¼	196¾	+ ¼	291½	194¼	174,960
Mr00	210½	211½	206	208½	....	270	206	35,171
May	215½	218	213¼	215	– ¼	261	213¼	5,073
July	221¾	223½	219	221¼	....	278½	219	7,601
Dec	237½	237½	232½	234¾	– ¼	279½	232½	5,726

Est vol 80,000; vol Fr 82,831; open int 338,004, +1,722.

Source: *The Wall Street Journal.*

EXHIBIT 4
Futures Price Quotations

Interest Rate

Treasury Bonds (CBT)—$100,000; pts. 32nds of 100%

	Open	High	Low	Settle	Chg	Lifetime High	Low	Open Interest
Mar	103–29	104–01	103–04	103–12	–	18116–20	95–13	174,963
June	103–12	103–16	102–18	102–26	–	19113–15	94–27	197,770
Sept	103–00	103–01	102–06	102–12	–	19112–15	94–10	10,040
Dec	102–09	102–15	101–25	101–31	–	19111–23	93–27	732
Mr96	...	...	...	101–19	–	19102–08	93–13	130

Est vol 410,000; vol Wed 515,658; op int 383,714, +1,910.

Source: *The Wall Street Journal.*

42

TECHNICAL ANALYSIS

Two basic approaches exist to forecasting futures prices: (1) technical analysis and (2) fundamental analysis (see Key 43). Fundamental analysis deals with the supply and demand of the physical commodity. Technical analysis is concerned with the study of the action of the futures markets. The key factors of interest to the technical analyst are the level and movement of futures prices, trading volume, and open interest. Most traders use a blend of the two approaches to maximize trading success.

Technical analysis is the attempt to predict future price movements in the futures market by analyzing the way prices have moved in the past. Technical analysts consider such factors as the monetary and fiscal policy of the government, economic environment, industry trends, and political events to be irrelevant in attempting to predict future prices. Their concern is with the historical movement of prices and trading volume.

In contrast, the fundamental analyst focuses upon the causes of price movements. In the commodity futures market, for example, the fundamentalist considers the effect of such variables as bumper crops and drought. In financial futures, factors of concern might be the current level of interest rates and trade deficits. In stock options, accounting data are critical to fundamental analysis.

It is a commonly held belief that fundamental analysis is superior to technical analysis in determining long-run trends, whereas technical analysis is better for predicting shorter trends and timing entry and exit of positions. Although technical analysts acknowledge that prices are ultimately rooted in fundamental factors, they say that it takes too long to process and evaluate supply-and-demand factors. Because technical analysts assume that all influences on market action are automatically accounted for or are discounted in price activity, it is the historical pattern of prices that should be evaluated rather than the many factors that determine supply and demand.

Technical analysts use a wide variety of techniques in attempting to predict futures prices. Many rely upon charts and look for particular configurations that are supposed to have predictive value. Entire books have been devoted to interpreting charts. Another style of technical analysis focuses upon volume, open interest, and the momentum of prices. Others use mechanical trading signals on an automatic basis.

Although the tools and techniques of technical analysis vary greatly, there are certain principles that underlie all forms of technical analysis:

1. Market value is entirely determined by the interaction of supply and demand.
2. Both rational and irrational factors govern supply and demand.
3. Prices tend to show patterns that persist for significant periods of time.
4. Changes in trends are caused by the shift in supply and demand.
5. Chart patterns tend to recur, and can be used to forecast future prices.
6. Shifts in supply and demand can be deduced in charts of market prices.

Although price is the indicator of greatest interest to technical analysts, volume and open interest are important secondary indicators. *Volume* is the number of contracts traded during a specified period of time—usually one day. Every time a trade occurs, volume increases. To determine the volume, sum the total of the short positions taken that day, or add the total of the long positions taken. The two should not be added together because each contract requires a buyer and a seller.

As a rule, volume is an indicator of the conviction behind a price movement. For example, a continuance of an upward trend is considered more likely when trading volume increases during rallies and dries up during declines. A lack of volume on the upside would mean that the upturn lacks conviction and the market is technically weakening. The opposite would occur in a bear market. In this case, trading volume should tend to increase during declines and slip when prices stage minor rallies.

Open interest is the total number of contracts outstanding or unliquidated at the end of the day. To determine the open interest in a market, add the number of short positions *or* long positions held at the close of the trading day (do not add the two together). Open interest increases when a new long buys from a new short; it decreases when an old long sells to an old short. However, open interest does not change when a new long buys from an old long or a new short sells to an old short. In this case, a new investor is simply replacing the old investor. The following chart summarizes the effect of transactions on open interest:

Buyer	Seller	Change in open interest
Buy new long	Sell new short	Increase
Buy new long	Sell old long	No change
Buy old short	Sell new short	No change
Buy old short	Sell old long	Decrease

Open interest is a valuable diagnostic tool because it measures the flow of money into the market. Increasing open interest means that money is flowing into the market and enhances the likelihood that the present trend will continue. A rise in open interest accompanied by rising prices means that buyers are the dominating force in the market. In other words, buyers are more aggressive than the sellers of new shorts. Alternatively, rising open interest combined with weakening prices is an indication that the short sellers are dominating the market and that prices will trend lower. Rising open interest tends to be a confirmation of the existing trend.

A fall in open interest while prices are rallying indicates that short sellers are dominating the market. The rise in prices is largely a reflection of the short sellers covering their positions. The rise in prices will last only as long as the shorts continue to cover their positions. When the shorts finally stop covering their positions, prices often will dip.

A price decline accompanied by falling open interest also suggests a temporary state. This condition suggests that the selling pressure is from the existing longs. After the existing longs have sold out, prices should rally. The following chart summarizes the interpretation of price, volume, and open interest:

Price	Volume	Open interest	Trend
Rising	Up	Up	Bullish
Rising	Down	Down	Weakening
Declining	Up	Up	Bearish
Declining	Down	Down	Strengthening

These guidelines are not meant to be hard-and-fast rules. Speculating is never that simple. For example, when interpreting open interest, one must consider seasonal factors. In the futures market, open interest is subject to seasonal changes that vary depending upon the nature of the underlying commodity or financial instrument.

Many mechanical trading systems have been developed by technical analysts. In most of these systems, software is used to process data and generate buy and sell signals. One type of mechanical trading system is the computation of *moving averages*. Moving averages are among the oldest trading tools and are easy to compute. A moving average is an average that is updated by dropping the first number and adding in the last number. The purpose of computing a moving average is to smooth out short-term rises and declines in prices and reveal the underlying trend. For example, suppose that the closing prices for a commodity over three days were: 60.50, 60.75, and 60.55.

Day 1	60.50
Day 2	60.75
Day 3	60.55
	181.80 ÷ 3 = 60.60

The average of the three prices is 60.60. Suppose that the price at the close of the fourth day is 60.35. In this case, the new three-day moving average would be computed as follows:

Day 2	60.75
Day 3	60.55
Day 4	60.35
	181.65 ÷ 3 = 60.55

The new three-day moving average is computed by eliminating the first day and adding the next three days together and dividing by 3. The decline in the closing price on the fourth day caused the moving average to fall from 60.60 to 60.55.

Any number of days can be used to compute a simple moving average. The shorter the moving average, the more sensitive it will be to price changes. The longer the number of days selected, the less responsive the average will be to price changes. A trading rule based upon a simple moving average is to be long when the daily closing price is above the moving average and short when the daily closing price is below the moving average.

This discussion barely scratches the surface of this complex and frequently arcane subject. For a good introduction to this subject, we recommend Jack Schwager's

Getting Started in Technical Analysis (John Wiley & Sons, 1995). Those investors who want a comprehensive guide to trading systems should consider Perry Kaufman's *Trading Systems and Methods* (John Wiley & Sons, 1998).

43

FUNDAMENTAL ANALYSIS

With commodities, all significant price moves are rooted in fundamental factors. Unless there is an actual shortage or surplus of the actual commodity, unusually low or high prices cannot be maintained. The aim of fundamental analysis is to recognize a developing imbalance between supply and demand and take a position in the futures market that will profit from the eventual price change this imbalance will cause.

The fundamental analyst estimates the supply of the commodity in the near future and the consequent demand. The supply of a commodity is the sum of imports, current production, and any carryover. Consumption or demand is determined by summing domestic use and exports. The fundamental analyst strives to determine and evaluate the factors that are likely to exert the greatest influence on the price of the commodity.

Factors other than local supply and demand also influence the price of a commodity, and these must be considered by the fundamental analyst. One of these influences is the *general commodity price level*. When the general commodity price level is unusually high or low, price levels in the other markets are affected. Shifts in the value of the U.S. currency vs. foreign currencies also exert an influence on commodity prices by changing the amount of the commodity that foreign buyers can get for their money. Other external market factors include:

- Production and price controls set by the government
- Actions taken by international trade organizations
- U.S. monetary and fiscal policy

- General condition of the economy

Also, the fundamental analyst must be aware of seasonal price tendencies. For example, Chicago December wheat reaches a summer low around July or August, and from this low, a seasonal price advance usually occurs into at least November or December. The fundamental analyst must be familiar with these seasonal tendencies and understand the causes responsible for these patterns.

Basic information on most active futures markets and commodities is readily available. The largest single source of information of this type is the federal government. The U.S. Department of Agriculture (www.usda.gov) publishes more than a hundred reports annually on farmers' growing intentions, projected yields, forecasted demand, and actual production of agricultural commodities. Other government agencies report on nonagricultural commodities, and on such important market influences as projected and actual imports, exports, weather, and legislative action. The Federal Reserve System (www.bog.fdr.fed.us and www.ny.frb.org) publishes a number of publications covering topics related to interest rates. In addition, there are many private crop and private forecasting services.

The Department of Agriculture publishes the useful pamphlet *How to Get Information from the U.S. Department of Agriculture,* which can be downloaded at www.usda/gov/news/howto.htm. This directory lists sources of information in the U.S. Department of Agriculture and its various agencies.

The Commodity Futures Trading Commission (CFTC) was created by Congress as an independent governmental agency with the mandate to regulate commodity futures and options markets. The CFTC (www.cftc.gov) issues several significant periodicals and special reports. *The Commitments of Traders Report* provides open interest in futures contracts by several categories. The CFTC also publishes an annual report that provides data and commentary.

Finally, the Futures Industry Association (FIA), the

trade association for the futures industry, issues weekly, monthly, and bimonthly publications that provide a constant flow of information on options and futures. *Market Beat* is a monthly newsletter featuring updates and proposals affecting the futures industry as well as trading volume statistics. *Futures Industry Magazine* is published seven times per year and provides comprehensive coverage on key issues and trends in derivative markets. This magazine is now available on line (www.fiafii.org and click on FIA Publications).

44

ROLE OF THE FEDERAL RESERVE BOARD

The Federal Reserve Board (Fed) is our central bank that oversees the activities of over 4,000 banks that are members of the Federal Reserve System. These member banks account for 60 percent of all commercial bank deposits. With its broad supervisory authority over these banks, the Fed controls the nation's money supply. Although the Fed does not control interest rates, it can significantly influence interest rates through its control of the money supply.

The Fed uses the following tools to manage the money supply:

1. *Open-market operations.* These operations, the most flexible policy instrument available to the Fed, consist of the purchase and sale of government securities (bills, notes, and bonds) on the open market. For example, when the Fed sells securities, it takes money out of the banking system. This action reduces the money supply, which puts upward pressure on interest rates. However, when the Fed buys securities, it injects money into the banking system. This loosening of the money supply reduces pressure on interest rates. These transactions are employed continuously each day as needed.

2. *Discount window.* Discounting occurs when the Fed lends reserves to member banks. The rate of interest the Fed charges is called the *discount rate.* The discount rate is altered periodically as market conditions change or to complement open market

operations. It is primarily of interest as an indication of the Fed's view of the economy and of credit demand.

3. *Reserve requirements.* Banks are required to maintain reserves against the money they loan. When the Fed increases reserve requirements, the amount of deposits supported by the supply of reserves is reduced and banks have to reduce the number of loans they make. This tool is the least flexible Fed instrument and is seldom used.

Because reserves are not interest-bearing deposits, it is in the interest of each bank to keep only the required minimum on deposit. Once the minimum reserve requirements are met, member banks can loan excess reserve funds, known as *fed funds*, to banks in need of additional cash. The financial community closely watches the fed funds rate because it is a short-term interest rate and generally acts as a benchmark for other short-term interest rates. Thus, changes in the fed funds rate have a definite influence on the prices of financial futures.

Futures Contract. Each business day, U.S. banks borrow from each other an average of approximately $100 billion in dollar deposits with a one-day term to maturity (overnight fed funds). The interest rate charged by banks with excess reserves to other banks needing overnight loans to meet their reserve requirements is called the *fed effective rate.* Because the rate is set daily by the market, it is a good indicator of the direction of interest rates. The fed effective rate is calculated and reported daily by the Federal Reserve Bank of New York, which computes the weighted average rate at which these interbank transactions are conducted.

The CBOT trades a fed funds futures contract based upon the overnight fed effective rate and one-month term fed funds rate. The CBOT 30-day Fed Funds Futures contract offers an effective hedging tool for any financial institution, bank, pension fund, corporation, or municipality that borrows or loans funds in the short-term market. Each contract has a face value of $5 million and the settlement price is calculated as 100 minus the average of the overnight fed effective rates for each calendar day of the month. For example, if the monthly average is 5.25, the futures settlement price is quoted as 94.75 (100 − 5.25).

Those investors desiring more information should request the booklet *Practical Applications Using CBOT Fed Funds Futures*, published by the CBOT (312-435-3500).

45

SPREADS

Most speculative futures transactions involve either buying futures with the expectation of benefiting from rising prices or selling futures with the expectation of benefiting from declining prices. However, numerous other strategies are available to futures participants. One relatively simple example is the use of spread positions.

A simple spread involves buying one futures contract and selling another futures contract in the same or economically related commodities. Prices of the two futures contracts have a tendency to go up and down together, and gains on one side of a spread are offset by losses on the other. The purpose of a spread is to profit from an expected change in the relationship between the purchase price of one and the selling price of the other. The Kansas City Board of Trade (KCBT), in its booklet *Wheat Futures*, provides an illustration of a spread.

EXAMPLE:
Suppose that a speculator expects corn prices to gain relative to hard red winter wheat prices because a severe summer drought is expected to reduce corn production. Currently, KCBT hard red winter wheat December futures are trading at a $.90 premium to December corn futures. If the speculator's expectations are borne out, the spread between corn and wheat prices will narrow. Therefore, on June 15, one December corn contract (5,000 bushels) is purchased at $3.10 and one December wheat contract (5,000 bushels) is sold at $4.00 for a spread of $.90. Suppose that by July 15, the December corn futures price has risen to $3.35 and the December wheat futures price has risen to $4.10. The spread has

narrowed to $.75, producing a profit of $.15:

	Wheat Transaction	Corn Transaction		Spread
June 15:				
Sell Dec	$4.00	—	=	$0.90
Buy Dec	—	$3.10		
July 15:				
Buy Dec	$4.10	—	=	$0.75
Sell Dec	—	$3.35		
Profit (loss)	($0.10)	$0.25	=	$0.15

Profit per contract = $0.15 × 5,000 bushels = $750

Note that because the spread moved in the expected direction, the profit from the corn transaction more than offset the loss from the wheat transaction. In trading spreads, individual price movement (up and down) is irrelevant. Profit or loss is determined only by the change in the relationship of the prices between the two commodities. Consequently, spreads often are considered more conservative and less risky than having an outright long or short futures position. Therefore, margins on spreads are lower than margins on outright purchases or sales of futures contracts.

46

DERIVATIVES

Over the last decade, the business press has devoted a great deal of attention to the risks posed by derivatives to the financial system. Awareness of these risks has been heightened by the large losses sustained by hedge funds, dealers, and some corporations that use derivatives to speculate on interest rates and currencies. Although derivative terminology can be daunting (see Exhibit 5 for an explanation of some basic terms), a broad definition is easy to grasp.

Derivatives are financial instruments with a value derived from fluctuations in the share of an underlying asset, such as share price, interest rate, or currency exchange rate. Derivatives can be based upon currencies, commodities, government or corporate debt, home mortgages, stocks, interest rates, or any combination of these. Options and futures are major classes of derivatives.

The risk of trading in derivatives became a worldwide concern in the summer and fall of 1998 because of huge losses sustained by hedge funds. U.S. hedge funds are unregulated private investment partnerships available only to qualified investors. Because they are private investment partnerships, the SEC limits hedge funds to 99 investors, at least 65 of whom must be "accredited." Accredited investors typically are defined as investors having a net worth of $1 million. Because managers generally receive about 20 percent of the profits but do not suffer losses, there is a tendency to assume increasing risks. Consequently, many hedge funds leverage their assets by buying derivatives that give them an exposure far greater than their capital.

The derivatives market is huge and incredibly complex.

The estimated volume of worldwide derivatives out-standing as of 1999 was at least $60 trillion in terms of the notional, or principal, amount of derivative contracts. The different types of derivative contracts can be confusing. There are now more than 1,200 different kinds of derivatives most of which require software to properly evaluate. In fact, pricing and trading derivatives would be impossible without sophisticated computer systems.

Although derivatives can be used for speculative purposes, the most common use is hedging. For example, companies often use forward (Exhibit 5) and exchange-listed futures to protect against fluctuations in currency or commodity prices.

Russia's default on its bonds in 1998 caused severe difficulties for several hedge funds that had made large investments in high-yielding, short-term Russian government debt in the mistaken expectation that the West would bail out Russia from its financial woes. When these bonds became almost worthless, hedge funds were forced to sell their other investments to meet margin calls. These forced sales caused a spectacular collapse in global markets. As a result, the DJIA dropped 19.3 percent in the 45-day period from July 17 to August 31, 1998.

The most publicized hedge fund failure was that of Long-Term Capital Management (LTCM). Its strategy was to exploit small valuation anomalies between various classes of bonds, dealing in bond derivatives called "total return swaps." When interest rates of bonds failed to converge as expected because of the Russian collapse, LTCM revealed in September 1998 that it had lost around $2 billion in the previous month. It also disclosed that its capital base had shrunk to less than $1 billion while its liabilities had ballooned to about $200 billion. Concerned about its possible collapse, the Federal Reserve Bank of New York arranged for a consortium of leading investment banks to inject $3.4 billion into LTCM in exchange for a 90 percent stake in the fund.

Forwards represent the largest component of the

derivatives market due to the need by businesses to reduce the uncertainty of variable costs, such as foreign currency transactions. For example, a U.S. importer might promise to buy machinery at a future date for a price quoted in Japanese yen. This importer can use a forward contract (or a futures contract, if one is available that meets the firm's needs) to fix the dollar cost of converting the Japanese yen at that future date. Thus, the importer avoids a loss if the dollar cost of Japanese yen increases between the purchase and delivery dates.

Derivatives are one of the cheapest and most effective tools a company has to protect itself against shocks in currency values, commodity prices, and interest rates. Over two thirds of the 500 largest U.S. companies use derivatives regularly according to a recent study. Companies use them as a kind of financial insurance policy, locking in currency or interest rate values for months or years, allowing companies to plan spending and operating budgets with some assurance.

Improperly used, however, derivatives can increase rather than reduce risk exposure. Derivative losses incurred by business firms, both from the United States and overseas, mutual funds, hedge funds, and even governments have heightened concerns over these financial instruments. Although increased regulation has been proposed, little has been accomplished. However, a likely outcome is that there will be a requirement for fuller financial statement disclosure of the risks assumed by the entities using these volatile instruments. Those desiring more information can check the interesting Web site run by the monthly magazine *Derivatives Strategy* (www.derivatives.com).

EXHIBIT 5
Derivatives Trading Language

Call: An option that gives the buyer the right to purchase a specified quantity of an asset at a fixed price at any time during the life of the option.

Cap: A contract that protects the holder from a rise in interest rates beyond a certain point.

Floor: A contract that protects the holder against a decline in prices below a certain point.

Forward: A contract obligating one party to buy, and the other party to sell, a specific asset for a fixed price at a future date.

Future: A contract between a buyer and seller specifying a commodity or financial instrument to be delivered and paid for at a future date. Unlike forward contracts, futures contracts are managed through an organized futures exchange.

Notional value: The full value of the obligations owed by all parties involved in a derivatives contract.

Put: An option that gives the buyer the right to sell a specified quantity of the underlying interest at a fixed price at any time during the life of the option.

Swap: An agreement by two parties to exchange a series of cash flows in the future.

Swaption: An option giving the holder the right to enter into or cancel a swap at a future date.

Underlying: The asset, index, or benchmark that determines the value of the derivative by its price movements.

47

OPENING A
FUTURES ACCOUNT

Futures and options on futures contracts are traded through brokerage firms. Therefore, the first step in trading futures is selecting a broker. This decision will be affected by the investor's experience in and knowledge of futures markets and the commitment in time and effort to be made in trading futures. Many futures traders prefer to do their own research and analysis and make their own decisions. In other words, they trade futures in a way that is similar to the management of their own stock portfolios. Other traders rely on the recommendations of a brokerage firm. Some traders purchase independent trading advice and make their decisions accordingly. Still others choose to participate in a commodity trading pool.

There is no magic formula for deciding how to participate in futures trading. The decision should be based on such factors as knowledge and experience in trading futures, the time and attention that will be devoted to trading, the amount of capital committed, and individual temperament and tolerance for risk. Some individuals thrive on the fast pace of futures trading; others are unable to make the immediate decisions that frequently are required. Some individuals accept the fact that futures trading usually results in losses; others lack the discipline to acknowledge a bad decision and liquidate a position.

The on-line trading of futures is a new dimension of this market. Some brokers (e.g., www.altavest.com) offer traders the ability to transmit on-line orders without interacting with a broker. In addition, the on-line broker-ages charge significantly lower fees, that is, $12 to $25 per round-turn contract rather than the $40 to $60 charged by a full-service broker. The fee for a *round-turn trade* means the charge is for both the purchase and sale of a futures contract. However, we recommend that inexperienced traders use a knowledgeable full-service broker. A full-service broker can prevent obvious mistakes (e.g., order placement) and help a novice understand the language of the markets. Paying an extra $30 can avoid a disastrous trade.

Opening an account with a broker is not significantly different from opening a bank account. A prospective investor must provide his/her name, address, occupation, social security number, citizenship, an acknowledgment that the customer is of legal age, and a suitable bank or financial reference. For futures traders, other information, such as financial data, is used to determine whether the individual is financially qualified to trade futures. In addition, every new account must sign a risk-disclosure statement that describes the risks associated with futures trading. If the broker does not strongly advise about risks, an alternative broker should be consulted.

Prospective customers also are required to sign a security-deposit statement. This agreement requires that a customer make good any losses incurred in trading. Funds deposited for margin requirements are required to be accounted for separately by a broker. By law, these segregated funds are not subject to liens against the broker. After the funds are deposited, trades can be made.

The amount of money needed to start futures trading varies with the type and quantity of contracts purchased. Funds must be adequate to pay the initial margin requirement and to meet possible margin calls to replenish the account. The broker will prescribe the initial margin requirement. Some brokers may ask for a customer deposit of $5,000, whereas others may require $25,000 or more.

48

TIPS ON TRADING FUTURES

Given the danger of trading futures, speculators should observe certain rules. The most important single characteristic of successful futures traders is that they are disciplined. They have a plan or system and they follow it. Those without a plan or system should not be in the business of futures trading. This market is not for casual investors. It is dominated by professionals who work full-time at searching for and exploiting opportunities.

Rules to follow in trading futures include the following:

1. *Select an experienced broker.* Trade only with a reputable firm that has at least one broker with extensive experience in trading futures. To select a broker, ask for the opinion of the office manager and then arrange for an interview. Determine that the broker has appropriate experience (at least three years) and qualifications to be of assistance. Investors should shop around until they find a broker with whom they feel comfortable.

2. *Set a maximum risk.* Decide the maximum acceptable loss. This loss can be expressed as a specific dollar amount or percentage of margin. Futures traders are likely to have more losses than gains. The key to success is to cut losses short and let profits run.

3. *A way to force discipline is to use stop orders.* A stop order is an order that becomes a market order when a particular price level is reached. A sell stop is placed below the market; a buy stop is placed above the market.

4. *Never meet a margin call.* When the initial margin is reduced by losses, the broker will call for a deposit of more margin. Instead of depositing more money, liquidate the position and accept the loss.

5. *Make dry runs for at least three months before actual money is risked.* This experience is vital for success as a futures trader. Many investors plunge into this market without adequate preparation and practice.

6. *Specialize in the futures markets.* Investors should specialize in only a few commodities or stock index futures. The more narrow the interest, the easier it is to become knowledgeable.

7. *Trade in futures only what can afford to be lost.* If the loss of this amount would cause loss of sleep, then investing in the futures market is not appropriate.

8. *Avoid overtrading.* If there are no opportunities, refrain from trading. At certain times futures should be avoided. Trading should occur only when the risk-to-reward ratio is acceptable.

9. *Risk no more than 10 percent of trading funds in any single position.* This limit will prevent the decimation of trading capital as a result of a bad trade.

10. *Never average down.* Do not buy more contracts when there is a loss in existing contracts.

49

INFORMATION ON FUTURES

Studies have shown that most speculators in futures lose money. Hence, this market is very risky. Investors who are not willing to spend a great deal of time studying this market should avoid it altogether. Trading in futures primarily is undertaken by individuals and professionals who may spend hours *each day* acquiring the expertise to make successful trades.

The exchanges where futures are traded are the first place to look for information on futures. All of these exchanges have brochures explaining how the exchange works, descriptions of the futures markets in general, and the contracts they trade in particular. Some brochures even offer suggestions on trading strategies. The Web sites and phone numbers of the major futures exchanges follow:

Chicago Board of Trade
www.cbot.com
312-435-3500

Chicago Mercantile Exchange
www. cme.com
312-930-1000

Kansas City Board of Trade
www.kcbt.com
816-753-7500

New York Futures Exchange
www.nyce.com
212-742-5050

New York Mercantile Exchange
www.nymex.com
212-748-3000

Several periodicals are excellent sources of information on futures. The financial weekly *Barron's* (800-822-7229) has a column "Commodities Corner," written by Cheryl S. Einhorn. This column is an excellent source of information on what is happening currently in the futures market.

An informative monthly magazine is *Futures,* which specializes in both futures and options. Its discussions of different trading techniques are particularly enlightening. A one-year subscription costs $39 (888-898-5514). *Futures* also maintains an excellent free Web site (www.futuresmag.com) that includes the latest issue of the magazine, daily updates with commentary on hot markets, a chat room, and links to relevant sites.

Most speculators in futures use technical analysis to determine the best time to make trades in futures (see Key 42). Technical analysis assumes that prices exhibit repetitive patterns and that the recognition of these patterns can be used to identify trading opportunities. With information on variables such as price, trading volume, and open interest, the technical analyst attempts to form an opinion about the future direction of prices. Technical analysts spend considerable time scrutinizing price charts and searching for patterns.

A useful monthly magazine for those interested in technical analysis is *Technical Analysis of Stocks and Commodities.* This monthly magazine, which costs $64.95 for a one-year subscription, is a publication for traders interested in the arcane techniques used by technical analysts. Futures traders should check out its Web site at www.traders.com.

The subject of futures can only be skimmed in a book of this size. Many excellent books are available that offer more comprehensive, technical treatment of futures and futures trading. Beginning investors might consider *Getting Started in Futures* by Todd Lofton (John Wiley & Sons, 1997). Another good book for the beginning investor is *The Electronic Futures Trader* by Jake Bernstein (McGraw-Hill, 1999). For more experienced investors, a comprehensive treatment is *The Futures Game* by Richard Teweles and Frank Jones (McGraw-Hill, 1999).

50

FUTURES ON LINE

The exchanges are the greatest single source of information about the futures contracts they trade and futures activity in the marketplace. Some of the features offered on the Web sites include price quotes, market commentary, volume and open interest, technical analysis, current cash prices for each commodity and index, background information on each futures market, contract specifications, crop reports, education, and news. Stated simply, the exchanges are an important and invaluable source of information, much of which is free of charge. The addresses for the major exchanges are provided below:

Chicago Board of Trade	www.cbot.com
Mid-America Commodity Exchange (wholly owned affiliate of CBOT)	www.cbot.com
Chicago Mercantile Exchange	www.cme.com
New York Mercantile Exchange	www.nymex.com
COMEX (a division of NYME)	www.nymex.com
New York Futures Exchange	www.nyce.com
Kansas City Board of Trade	www.kcbt.com

Some of the discount futures brokers provide a wide variety of free futures information. The largest, Lind-Waldock (www.lindwaldock.com), has a web-based trading system that offers user-friendly interface, easy navigation, drop-down menus, customizable quote and order entry pages, real-time account status, and other desirable features. An interesting feature is a squawk box that provides live audio commentary direct from the S&P pit of the Chicago Mercantile Exchange.

Customers of the firm are allowed 500 free, real-time price quotes per month with additional quotes costing

$0.05 each. In addition, click on "Trader's Catalog" to obtain an extensive list of books, publications, and services focused on futures trading that account holders can purchase at a discount. Finally, Lind-Waldock lets a customer experience what it is like to trade an account on line without actually entering the market and risking any capital. Simulated on-line trading can be practiced on all major domestic and international exchange-traded futures and options contracts.

TFC Commodity Futures & Financial Market Charts (www.tfc-charts.w2d.com) is probably the best free chart service available on the Internet. TFC tracks many commodities and financial indicators, making the information available in the form of daily, weekly, and monthly charts. With the charts is included an analysis of certain key indicators, such as open interest, relative strength index, and short-, medium-, and long-term moving averages. A personalized charts menu can be created to gain quick access to the charts of greatest interest to a trader.

INO.com (www.ino.com) bills itself as the "largest and most comprehensive Web site for futures and options traders." This attractive site tracks a wide variety of options and futures. Free intraday, daily, and weekly charts of individual contracts at various exchanges are provided. Prices and graphs of "extreme" (biggest) winners and losers for both futures and stocks are presented and updated throughout the trading day every 15 minutes.

FutureSource (www.futuresource.com) is another comprehensive site with delayed quotes, charts, news, and market updates. Also provided are links to other futures-related sites and subscription-based sources. An interesting feature is the detailing of stops on various futures contracts. Most traders who establish buy or sell stops in futures markets do so based upon chart patterns or psychological price levels. This site provides its estimate of where these stops are located for a wide variety of contracts.

QUESTIONS AND ANSWERS

Why have stock index futures become so popular with institutional and individual investors?

Trading in stock index futures began in 1982 when the Kansas City Board of Trade introduced a futures contract on the Value Line Composite Index. Today, the two main stock index futures contracts traded in the United States are (1) Standard & Poor's (S&P) 500 contract at the Chicago Mercantile Exchange (by far the most popular index futures contract) and (2) Mini S&P 500 contract traded on the same exchange.

Investors have found stock index futures contracts to be an efficient vehicle for trading on expectations of general movements in the equity market. Stock index futures permit investors to participate in broad market movements without having to individually acquire hundreds of different stocks. Index futures also enable investors to hedge their portfolios against short-term losses by selling futures short. This strategy often is preferable to disrupting the portfolio by temporarily selling off individual stocks.

What are some of the basic positions that can be assumed when trading futures?

Three principal strategies to employ in trading futures are to (1) "go long," (2) "go short," and (3) "spread." Going long means buying a futures contract in anticipation of a price increase. The opposite of going long is going short, which means selling a futures contract in

141

anticipation of a price decrease. A spread position is the simultaneous purchase and sale of futures contracts in different months, or in different markets, hoping that a price differential between the two will result in a profit.

Positions in the futures market are closed out by taking the opposite action of the initial position. Thus, a long position is closed out by a sale of the same contract month, a short position is liquidated by a purchase of the same contract month, and a spread position is eliminated by simultaneously buying and selling in the opposite way to the initial action.

What is the significance of daily price limits for futures?

Each exchange sets limits within which a future's price can fluctuate during a single trading session. This restriction serves to limit the exposure of traders on any single trading day. The exchange determines the price ranges based upon variations occurring in the underlying cash markets. These ranges can be adjusted periodically as price volatility increases or decreases. In some contracts, daily price limits are eliminated during the month in which the contract expires. Prices are particularly volatile during the expiration month. As a result, inexperienced traders may wish to liquidate prior to that time.

The limits are expressed in terms of the previous day's closing price plus or minus an amount per trading unit. When a futures price has risen by its daily limit, there can be no trading at any higher price until the next day of trading. Alternatively, when a futures price has declined by its daily limit, there can be no trading at any lower price until the next day of trading. Therefore, if the daily limit for a particular grain is currently $0.10 per bushel and the previous day's settlement price was $3.50, no trading can occur during the current day at any price below $3.40 or above $3.60. The price is allowed to increase or decrease only by the limit amount each day.

How can options be used to hedge against a decline in the market price of common stock?

Two common strategies are (1) covered call writing and (2) buying puts. Covered call writing involves writing calls against common stock already owned. Premiums earned from writing call options provide both cash flow and price protection. The protection from a decline in the price of the common stock is limited to the amount of the premium.

The other common hedging strategy involves the purchase of put options. Speculative stocks typically involve greater risk in the pursuit of large profits. Buying put options reduces the risk of acquiring such stocks while still maintaining the upside potential of the stock.

What are the major variables influencing options premiums?

An at-the-money option (price of the common stock equals the exercise price) has the greatest time value. An out-of-the-money option has less time value because there is less likelihood of profitably exercising the option. Because of the reduced opportunity for leverage, a substantially in-the-money option also has less time value. Its premium is predominantly a reflection of its intrinsic value.

An option is a "wasting asset" because it has no value after expiration. An option's time value and premium are influenced by the length of time remaining until expiration. Therefore, the longer the time remaining, the greater the time value.

The volatility of the underlying common stock also affects the option premium. The more volatile the price of the underlying common stock, the greater the option premium. If other factors remain unchanged, a substantial increase in the volatility of the underlying common stock will expand an option's premium.

Ultimately, option premiums are determined by the

forces of supply and demand. The supply results from the willingness of traders and investors to write (or sell) options, and the demand stems from the interest of other traders and investors in buying options. Not surprisingly, the demand for call options normally climbs when stock prices are rising and the demand for put options normally jumps when stock prices are slipping.

What are the similarities and dissimilarities of options as compared to stocks?

Options share certain similarities with common stocks. Among these are the following:

1. Both options and stock investors can follow price movements, trading volume, and other significant information day by day or even minute by minute. The buyer or seller of an option, like the buyer or seller of common stock, can learn almost instantly the price at which an order has been executed.
2. Both options and common stocks are listed securities. Orders to buy and sell options are transacted through brokers in the same way as orders to buy and sell common stock. In addition, orders are executed on the trading floor of a national, SEC-regulated exchange in an open, competitive auction market.

Some important differences exist between options and common stocks:

1. Options differ from common stocks in that they are "wasting assets." Common stock can be held indefinitely in anticipation of increased value. If an option is not closed out or exercised prior to its expiration date, it is worthless and the holder loses the entire premium.
2. Unlike common stock, there are no certificates evidencing ownership. Instead, positions in options are indicated on printed statements prepared by

brokerage firms.

3. Unlike shares of common stock, there is not a fixed number of options available. The number of outstanding options is determined by the number of buyers and sellers interested in receiving and selling these rights.

4. Common stock ownership provides the owner with an interest in the company, voting rights, and rights to any dividends distributed. However, an option owner's potential benefit is defined solely by possible movement in the price of a stock.

What does margin mean in the context of futures?

Every futures trader should understand two margin-related terms: (1) initial margin and (2) maintenance margin. Initial margin is the cash that must be deposited with the broker for each futures contract as a guarantee of the fulfillment of the contract. If profits accrue on an open futures position, the profits are added to the balance in a margin account. If losses accrue on a given day, the losses are deducted from the balance in a margin account.

If the balance in a margin account is reduced below a certain level (known as the "maintenance margin"), a broker will require the deposit of additional funds to bring the account back to its initial margin. Requests for additional margin are known as margin calls.

Each exchange sets its own rules for maintenance margin. Generally, additional margin is required when an unfavorable price movement has reduced the initial margin in the position down to 60 to 75 percent of its original value. Maintenance margin calls must be met promptly. If a margin call is not met, the customer's position can be liquidated to meet the margin call.

What are the different types of spreads in futures trading?

A spread is the simultaneous purchase and sale of futures

contracts for the same commodity or instrument for delivery in different months, or in different but related markets. The simplest spread is the simultaneous purchase of a long position in one futures contract and short position in a different but related futures contract. Spreads are established to profit from a change in the difference between the prices of the two contracts. Because gains and losses occur only as the result of a change in the price difference rather than changes in the absolute prices of the futures contracts, spreads usually are more conservative and less risky than having an outright long or short futures position.

There are three basic types of spreads:

1. *Intramarket spread.* This spread is the most common and consists of a long position in one contract month and a short position in a different contract month of the same commodity on the same exchange. An example of an intramarket spread is long December corn/short March corn on the Chicago Board of Trade.
2. *Intermarket spread.* This spread involves buying futures contracts on one exchange and selling the same contract on another exchange. An example is long wheat on the Chicago Board of Trade and short wheat on the Kansas City Board of Trade.
3. *Intercommodity spread.* This spread involves a long position in one commodity and a short position in a related commodity. An example is long oats/short corn.

What is the role of the Options Clearing Corporation?

Standardized options are issued by the Options Clearing Corporation (OCC), an agency regulated by the Securities and Exchange Commission (SEC). The OCC guarantees that the terms of an options contract will be fulfilled. An options buyer looks to the OCC rather than to any particular options writer for performance. In a similar vein, the obligations of options writers are owed to the OCC rather than to any particular buyer.

When there are matching orders from a buyer and seller, the OCC severs the link between the parties. In effect, the OCC guarantees contract performance by becoming the buyer to the seller and the seller to the buyer. As a result, the seller can buy back the same option he/she has written, and this action has no effect on the rights of the original buyer to sell, hold, or exercise his/her option.

What is program trading?

Program trading is a market strategy used by institutions to buy or sell vast amounts of securities. Typically, computers are programmed to evaluate the difference between the prices of actual stocks and the prices of futures contracts on an index made up of those stocks. If the futures rise to a premium over the aggregate value of the stocks on the index, the trader can sell the futures short and buy the underlying securities, exploiting the price differential between the two. The process is reversed when the futures sell at a discount to the stocks making up the index.

For example, if the price of the S&P 500 futures contract skids substantially below the market price of the stocks that make up the index, computers trigger automatic signals to sell stocks and buy the futures. If the prices of the S&P 500 stocks lag behind the futures on the index, the computer program will signal to buy these stocks and sell the futures to exploit the spread. As a rule, the futures sell at a premium to the cash index, especially in bull markets. Because stock prices have risen over the years (on average), the expectation of speculators in futures is for generally rising markets. Near the expiration date, the futures and the cash index are almost equal in value.

GLOSSARY

American-style option an option that can be exercised by the holder at any time after it is purchased until it expires.

At-the-money option an option with an exercise price equal to the price of the underlying common stock.

Basis the difference between the futures price and the current cash price of a commodity or security.

Bear one who believes that prices are headed lower.

Bear spread an investing position that involves the purchase of an option with a lower exercise price and the sale of an option with a higher exercise price.

Call option an option that gives the buyer the right to purchase a specified quantity of the underlying interest at a fixed price at any time during the life of the option.

Cap a contract that protects the holder from a rise in interest rates beyond a certain point.

CBOE (Chicago Board Options Exchange) the world's largest options exchange.

CBOT (Chicago Board of Trade) the world's largest futures exchange.

CME (Chicago Mercantile Exchange) the second largest futures exchange in the world.

Commodity futures a contract covering the purchase and sale of physical commodities for future delivery on a commodity exchange.

Contract month the month a contract matures; the delivery month.

Cover the closing out of a short position.

Covered call writing the writing of a call by someone who owns the shares of stock on which a call has been written.

Deep-in/out-of-the-money options a call option with a strike price that is significantly below the market price of the underlying stock (deep-in-the-money option) or significantly above the market price (deep-out-of-the-money option). The definition would be exactly the opposite for a put option.

Delta a measure of the change in an option's price compared to the change in the underlying price of the stock.

Derivative instruments financial instruments with a value derived from the stocks, bonds, indexes, currencies, and so on, on which they are based.

European-style option an option that may be exercised only on the expiration date.

Exercise price the price at which the holder can sell to or buy from the writer the item underlying an option.

Financial futures a futures contract that involves the delivery of financial securities or cash to fulfill the contract.

Firm-specific risk risk that results from factors peculiar to an individual company.

Floor a contract that protects the holder against a decline in prices below a certain point.

Floor broker an exchange member who executes trades for the accounts of others.

Fundamental analysis prediction of future prices based upon an analysis of supply and demand.

Future an agreement between two parties that commits one party to sell a commodity or security to the other at a given price and on a specified future date.

Hedging the purchase and sale of options and futures solely for the purpose of establishing a known price level.

Industry risk the risk that results from developments unique to an industry.

In-the-money options a call is in the money when the exercise price is less than the market price; a put is in the money when the exercise price is greater than the market price.

Intrinsic value the amount of money, if any, that could be realized by exercising the option.

LEAPS (Long-term Equity Anticipation Securities) options on individual stocks and indexes that provide the owner the right to purchase or sell shares of a stock at a specified price on or before a given date up to three years in the future.

Limit the maximum amount a futures price may move, up or down, in any one trading session.

Limit order a trade that can be executed only at a specific price.

Liquidation the closing out of a long position.

Long the purchase of a futures contract to establish a market position that has not been closed out through an offsetting sale; the opposite of short.

Maintenance margin the amount of money that must be maintained on deposit while a futures position is open.

Margin in futures trading, a good faith deposit to guarantee fulfillment of the purchase or sale obligation.

Margin call a demand for additional cash because of an unfavorable movement in price.

Market order an order stipulating that a trade should be executed at the best price currently available.

Market risk the risk that results from overall movements of the market.

Moving average an average that is updated by dropping the earliest value and adding in the most recent value.

Naked option same as uncovered option.

Open interest the number of contracts outstanding or unliquidated at the end of the day.

Option a contract that provides to its holder (buyer) the right to purchase from or sell to the issuer (writer) a specified interest at a designated price, called the strike price, for a given period of time.

Options buyer or holder the investor who obtains the right specified in an options contract.

Options on futures options that give the buyer the right, but not the obligation, to buy or sell a specific futures contract at a stated price at any time prior to a specified date.

Options writer the seller or issuer of an options contract.

Out-of-the-money option a call is out of the money when the exercise price is greater than the market price; a put is out of the money when the exercise price is lower than the market price.

Point the minimum price fluctuation of a contract.

Position an interest in the market in the form of open contracts, either long or short.

Premium the price paid by the buyer of an option to the seller of an option.

Program trading a mechanical trading system in which computers are programmed to buy or sell vast amounts of securities.

Protective puts the simultaneous purchase of a stock and a put option or the purchase of a put related to a stock already owned by the investor.

Put option an option that gives the buyer the right to sell a specified quantity of the underlying interest at a fixed price at any time during the life of the option.

Short a futures contract sold to establish a market position that has not been closed out through an offsetting purchase; the opposite of long.

Speculating assuming the price risk that hedgers are seeking to minimize.

Spreads the purchase and sale of options on the same underlying stock but with a different expiration date and/or a different exercise price.

Stop order an order to buy or sell at the market when a specific price is reached, either above or below the price that prevailed when the order was given.

Straddle the simultaneous purchase of a put and a call on the same stock with the identical expiration price and expiration month.

Strike price same as exercise price.

Swap an agreement by two parties to exchange a series of cash flows in the future.

Technical analysis attempts to predict future price movements by analyzing the past sequence of prices, volume, and so forth.

Tick same as point.

Time value the amount of money buyers are willing to pay for an option in the expectation that sometime before it expires it will become profitable to exercise or sell.

Uncovered call writing an options trading strategy in which the investor does not own the shares of the common stock represented by the option.

Uncovered option option contract in which the owner does not hold the underlying investment.

Uncovered put writing an options strategy in which the investor does not have a corresponding short stock position or has deposited cash or cash equivalents equal to the exercise value of the put.

Writer someone who sells an option.

INDEX